SOUTHGATE VETERANS
MEMORIAL LIBRARY
14680 DIX-TOLEDO ROAD
SOUTHGATE, MI 48195

P9-DNB-152
3 9082 11307 0414

Ernie Harwell

Stories From
My Life in Baseball

DATE DUE

MAR 17 2010

MAY 31 2011

SEP 0 3 2013

JUN 22 2016

14A

SOUTHGATE VETERANS
MEMORIAL LIBRARY
14680 DIX-TOLEDO ROAD
SOUTHGATE, MI 48195

Credits

Editors: Alison Boyce and Carlos Monarrez

Designer: Christoph Fuhrmans

Production editor: Bob Ellis

Copy editing: Bob Ellis, Ken Kraemer, Tim Marcinkoski, Shelly Solon and the Free Press sports copy desk

Cover photography: Andy Greenwell, www.greenwellphoto.com

Back cover photography: Ernie Harwell Collection

Sports editor: Gene Myers

Design and graphics director: Steve Dorsey

Project coordinator: Dave Robinson

Special thanks: Laurie Delves

Detroit Free Press

600 W. Fort St.
Detroit, Mich. 48226
www.freep.com

© 2001 by Detroit Free Press.
All rights reserved.
Manufactured by Malloy Lithographing.

No part of this book may be reproduced or transmitted in any form or by any means, electronic or mechanical, including photocopying, recording or by an information storage system, without permission of the publisher, except where permitted by law.

Other recent books by the Free Press:

The Detroit Almanac	HeartSmart Kids Cookbook
State of Glory	Corner to Copa
The Corner	Century of Champions
PC@Home	Yaklennium
Believe!	Stanleytown

To order any of these titles, please call 800-245-5082 or go to **www.freep.com/bookstore**
To subscribe to the Free Press, call 800-395-3300.

Other books by Ernie Harwell:

Tuned to Baseball	Diamond Gems
The Babe Signed My Shoe	

Ernie Harwell | Stories From My Life in Baseball
ISBN 0-937247-35-9
$14.95

Dedication

With deep appreciation for his insightful support and his constant loyalty, I dedicate this book to my friend and counselor, S. Gary Spicer.

When the folks at the Free Press first talked to me about this book, someone mentioned that its title might be "The Best of Ernie Harwell." Immediately I said, "No. That won't do. Any book has to be more than a page and a half!"

I want to thank those who were able to dig up 86 columns and put them into this collection. Special thanks go to: Dave Robinson, Carlos Monarrez, Alison Boyce, Christoph Fuhrmans, Gene Myers and Bob Ellis.

ERNIE HARWELL was born in Washington, Ga., on Jan. 25, 1918. He began his career in radio and television in 1940 and has been broadcasting major league baseball since 1948. The 2001 baseball season will be his 41st broadcasting Detroit Tigers games. Harwell has written three other books — "Tuned To Baseball," "Diamond Gems" and "The Babe Signed My Shoe" — and has written a baseball column regularly for the Detroit Free Press since 1991. He lives in Farmington Hills, Mich., with his wife, Lulu.

Table of Contents

For Openers

Ernie Harwell Collection

I got my start at WSB in Atlanta in 1940 when I auditioned for the sports announcer job and got lucky. I've been calling games ever since.

From the press box to the broadcast booth

This is a confession. I'm a failed sports writer. When I was a youngster, my ambition was to be a major league baseball player. Playing sandlot and college ball, I discovered that I would never make it. So I opted for writing.

With a change in ambition, I also changed my heroes. The stars of the diamond gave way to the big-time writers. I looked up to Grantland Rice, H.G. Salsinger, Paul Gallico and others.

When I was still in high school, I wrote a letter to the editor of the Sporting News, suggesting I be his paper's Atlanta correspondent. Not realizing I was only 16, he gave me the job. That same year, 1934, I began to work for Ralph McGill, sports editor of the Atlanta Constitution, doing menial jobs nobody else wanted.

That summer, I had my first contact with a big-league sports writer. I went to Chicago on vacation and took a letter from McGill introducing me to Ed Burns, the baseball expert of the Chicago Tribune. I was an avid reader of Burns' dispatches to the Sporting News, and he was somewhat an idol of mine.

I approached this newspaper shrine with great respect. But when I got off the elevator and reached the sports department, I saw a strange sight. Several sports writers were dancing around the room, trying to blow a Ping-Pong ball out of a tube and onto the wall — a frenzied, crazy game for a group of grown-ups.

That was my introduction to big-league sports writers.

Later, in Atlanta, I used to see the New York writers come through town with the barnstorming New York Yankees. One spring I saw the venerable Dan Daniel and the dignified Charlie Segar chase one of the Atlanta Crackers' secretaries around her desk during a spirited water-pistol fight.

Once I had seen my writer heroes in action, I realized that sports writing wasn't all work. I decided I wanted a job like theirs.

However, I was sidetracked. During my senior year at Emory University, I couldn't land a newspaper job in Atlanta. In May of that year (1940), I auditioned at radio station WSB to be its sports announcer. I got lucky. I won that job. And except for four years in the Marines during World War II, I've been in radio or television ever since.

Originally printed on June 29, 2000

3 9082 11307 0414

4

Beyond the Playing Field

Easley earned A's in getting-hit drill

D amion Easley gave his body to science when he was only 17 years old.

No, his heart won't be probed by medical researchers 200 years from now. And his brain won't be preserved in a laboratory jar for future examination. The Tigers second baseman turned his body over to the active, arcane artistry of getting hit by a pitch.

Easley's baseball coach at Long Beach City College in California, Ken Gaylord, specialized in teaching that particular science.

"Coach Gaylord made us stand at the plate," Easley recalled. "And he would throw at us. Every position player was required to go through that drill after each practice. He taught us to turn toward the pitch and let the pitches hit us on the meat part of our bodies. Sometimes he wouldn't throw right at us. Instead, he would throw inside and tell us to move into the pitch, allowing it to hit us. We would line up at the batting cage and go through the drill three or four times. And we'd always get hit. I did that drill for both of my two years at City College."

The best place to be hit?

"On the rear, without a doubt," Easley said. "The upper arm is good, or the thigh. I was skeptical about that drill when I first heard of it. But I feel now that it really helped me."

The course has paid off. Easley is one of the leading major-leaguers in the black-and-blue division of hit by pitch. He shares the major league record for being hit by a pitch three times in a game. Several have reached that painful pinnacle, but only two Tigers. It happened to Bill Freehan on Aug. 16, 1968, at Boston. And Easley was plunked three times May 31, 1999, also at Fenway Park.

Freehan is the Tigers' single-season leader in the hit-by-pitch department. His record is 24, set in 1968. Easley reached his high of 16 in 1998.

Some hit-by-pitch experts wear protection. Mo Vaughn, the American League leader with 13, encases his front arm with a plastic sheath to lessen the blows. Ron Hunt, who holds the major league record for being hit by most pitches in one season (50), wore a loose uniform with protection underneath, much like a flak jacket.

Easley eschews that sort of equipment. He depends on his training at City College, when he majored in Hit By Pitch 101.

Originally printed on Sept. 15, 2000

Tape trick
is a story that sticks

Reporter to New York Giants rookie, circa 1920: "Are you married?"
Rookie: "You'll have to ask Mr. McGraw."
This terse exchange illustrates the control and power a big-league manager once wielded over his players. Today, it is different. Managers and coaches are not complete masters over their charges anymore. A new technique is required.

Here, for example, is a story a modern big-league coach told me about how he corrected one of his players (not wanting to reveal the player's identity, I've given him a false name):

"We had a shortstop named George Zender who was playing awful. He couldn't concentrate. My manager told me to work with him.

"A big-leaguer doesn't want to be taught. Your presentation has to make the player think it's his idea. You can't say, 'This is the way to do it' or 'I have a suggestion for you.' The player won't listen. If I tell him he's not concentrating, he'll just blow me off. He'll say: 'I've been playing this game 18 years and I know what I'm doing. Leave me alone.'

"So here's what I do.

"I know exactly when George comes to the ballpark every day. I make it a point for three straight days to walk by him with two videotapes in my hand. I say, 'Hi, George,' and keep walking. On the fourth day, George can't contain his curiosity. 'What are you doing?' he asks me.

" 'I've got these tapes of you in action,' I tell him. 'One when you won your Gold Glove. The other for your last few games. I can't find anything wrong with the way you're fielding the ball.'

" 'I told you, there's nothing wrong,' George says.

" 'It's not really worth showing to you,' I tell him.

" 'Oh, come on, tell me,' he says.

" 'Well, when you won your Gold Glove,' I explain, 'you always looked at the ball a little bit longer after you fielded it. Now you're lifting your head too soon before you throw. But it's so close you really can't tell the difference.'

" 'Oh, yeah?' he says. 'I bet I can tell the difference.'

"Now I can show him the videos. He takes a look and tells himself he has discovered his flaw. He makes the correction and begins to play better.

"I have accomplished my purpose in three ways:

"1. I didn't burden him with a lot of teaching about mechanics.

"2. I gave him an excuse he could adopt as his own.

"3. I told him to concentrate without mentioning the word.

"Let me make a confession. I never looked at those videos. I sat in the video room for three days with the lights off. If George had ever checked the room, he would have discovered my web of intrigue."

Originally printed on July 1, 2000

Home run hitters proved me wrong

OK. For all those years, I was wrong.

The Home Run Chase of 1998 has forced me to change my idea about the drawing power of position players.

I used to contend that only star pitchers could increase attendance. Mark McGwire and Sammy Sosa have changed my mind.

During my 50-plus years of major league broadcasting, the top gate attractions have been pitchers. Bob Feller was the first. Then came Sandy Koufax, Mark Fidrych and Fernando Valenzuela. My theory was that since position players are in action every day, they don't have one special day to draw fans. But the super pitchers are on display every five days, making them special attractions.

Fidrych was the prime example. When he was the toast of baseball for the Tigers in 1976, opponents — even if they knew he might beat them — welcomed his appearance at their home games. He meant an extra 20,000 to 30,000 tickets sold each time he pitched.

The California Angels did something with the Bird I have seen only once. They staged an autograph session for a visiting player in their own park. Fidrych was stationed at a table behind home plate at the Big A, and a continuous line of fans weaved from centerfield around to home plate, where he signed for more than an hour. I'm not sure he was paid extra for signing. If he was, it probably wasn't any large amount.

Closest to the Bird as a gate attraction was Valenzuela. Whenever he pitched, he turned Dodger Stadium into a fiesta.

Feller and Koufax were Hall of Famers and commanded tremendous respect. But they didn't have the gate appeal of Fidrych and Valenzuela.

The only home run hitter I saw who put customers into the seats was Pittsburgh Pirates outfielder Ralph Kiner. But his drawing power didn't match that of Sosa's and McGwire's. During the late '40s and early '50s, when Kiner was on a home run tear, fans packed Forbes Field to watch an otherwise miserable team.

After the Hall of Famer took his apparent last at-bat of the game, fans would stream for the exits.

Now McGwire and Sosa have burst onto the scene to prove that the non-pitcher can pack 'em in. They have certainly discredited my old theory about gate attractions.

Originally printed on Sept. 12, 1998

Silent Murray
always delivered

One of the 1996 baseball season's great stories was Eddie Murray's 500th career home run. Coupled with his 3,000 hits, his accomplishment put Murray into the spotlight he had always tried to avoid.

Murray is quiet; he shuns outsiders. Among his teammates, he was always popular and a true leader other players looked to for guidance.

In his earlier years, Murray was cooperative with the media. Later, Dick Young, the late New York sports columnist, wrote something about Eddie's family that Murray resented. He turned against the media in general and refused to be interviewed.

I knew Eddie from the start of his career, and he was always pleasant toward me. Until the latter stages of his baseball lifetime, I did many interviews with him. As he grew cool to the media, I respected his viewpoint and didn't bother him.

I say all of this to lead into a strange story. On March 7, 1991, the Tigers opened their spring exhibition season against the Los Angeles Dodgers at Vero Beach, Fla. Our broadcast booth was on top of the old wooden stands. To reach the booth, you had to come up a long, rickety stairway. There were fans all around, and on this particular spring afternoon the stands were packed.

In the third inning of my broadcast, a large man

in a Dodgers uniform loomed at the door of the booth. He tapped lightly on the door and entered.

The man in uniform was Eddie Murray.

I could have expected a lot of people to come to our booth — newspaper people, politicians, sponsors, baseball executives, fans, even players. But the last man I would ever look for would be Eddie Murray.

Yet, there he was — The Silent One, the man who never communicated with the media.

"Ernie," he said, "some fan downstairs gave this to me and asked me to deliver it to you."

"Thanks, Eddie," I told him.

He walked away and carefully descended the old wooden steps to the field. I looked at the note he had brought. It was a request from a fan to say hello to his folks back home in Monroe.

The note didn't surprise me. But I still haven't recovered from the fact that it was delivered by Eddie Murray.

Originally printed on Oct. 12, 1996

International house of pitchers

Los Angeles Dodgers pitching coach Dave Wallace must now realize that when he attended the University of New Haven, his scholastic journey took a wrong turn.

Instead of majoring in business administration, he should have concentrated on languages. He oversaw a Dodgers pitching staff that almost outdid the United Nations in its ethnic diversity.

The starters on Wallace's Los Angeles 1996 staff were Hideo Nomo, a native of Osaka, Japan; Chan Ho Park, from Kong Ju City, Korea; Pedro Astacio, from Hato Mayor, Dominican Republic; Ismael Valdes, from Victoria, Mexico; and Ramon Martinez, from Santo Domingo, Dominican Republic.

If any of these got into trouble, Wallace could summon Antonio Osuna, a native of Sinaloa, Mexico.

All of which emphasizes the fact that language can be a problem. Wallace knew a smattering of Spanish, Japanese and Korean.

"Everybody from every country knows words like strike, ball, curve, hit-and-run and bunt," he said. "But sometimes communication gets a lot more complicated than that."

Wallace ran into one of those situations with Park, his right-hander from Korea.

"Park was pitching well in a particular game," Wallace recalled. "But then the opposition began to pick up a few hits off him. He began to get mad at himself. He lost his cool.

"I went out to talk to him and try to calm him down. He listened, and nodded his head in agreement. But he was still mad at himself. He never recovered his poise."

After the game, Wallace had another conversation with his Korean pitcher. "You're a good pitcher," Wallace told him. "But you get upset too easily. You must work on your emotions."

Park nodded in agreement as he listened to his pitching coach. Wallace was certain that the message was received. Three days later, Park came back to Wallace.

"I'm ready now for that extra work," he told the coach. "When do you start helping me with my motion?"

Wallace smiled and again reminded himself that when language nuances are involved, it's difficult to make yourself clear. Motion and emotion are close, but not the same.

Originally printed on Aug. 9, 1996

One and done for these managers

U ntil July 7, 1996 had been a good year for managers. It looked as if no manager would be fired before the All-Star Game for the first time since 1976.

Then the Florida Marlins dismissed Rene Lachemann, again proving that managers are hired to be fired . . . or they quit before the ax falls.

I remember two managers who walked away in a hurry.

Eddie Sawyer led the Philadelphia Phillies to a pennant in 1950, his third year on the job. That was the season of the "Whiz Kids."

But they were one-year wonders. After the pennant, Sawyer's team dropped into the second division the next season. By 1959, the Phillies were in the basement — even with a second baseman named George (Sparky) Anderson, who played all but three of his team's 155 games and hit .218 with no home runs and 34 RBIs.

Sawyer got through spring training in 1960. But he quit after a loss on Opening Day, and the Phils finished last without him. His resignation is the earliest managerial change in history.

Sawyer was a stout, grayhaired, friendly man. I enjoyed sitting in the dugout and chatting with him when I broadcast for the Dodgers and Giants. He had a fabulous memory, the best I've encountered in baseball. Ask him about any players or play, and he would astound you.

"Yes, I remember that play," he'd say. "It was the last of the sixth, Jim Hearn was pitching. We had (Mike) Goliat on first and two out, and the Giants were leading us, 2-0. Hearn threw a curve down and away, and (Bill) Nicholson hit it out of the park."

Why Sawyer quit after that one game in 1960, I never found out.

Another one-game manager was my old pal Eddie Stanky. We were very close when he played second base for the New York Giants in 1950-51.

In 1952, Eddie became the St. Louis Cardinals' manager and held that job through 1955. After coaching, he came back to manage the White Sox in 1966-68. He quit the pro ranks to become baseball coach at South Alabama.

In 1977, Eddie came out of retirement. Texas fired manager Frank Lucchesi on June 22 and hired Eddie. Stanky flew from Alabama to Minnesota and took over the team, and Texas beat the Twins that night. Eddie returned to his hotel room and called his wife, Dickie.

"I've had it," he told her. "One game of managing is enough for me. I'm coming home."

Stanky, one of the four Texas managers that year, was 1-0. That was the last game he ever managed.

Originally printed on July 18, 1996

Time catches Fisk, a past hero at-large

This is a sad time for Carlton Fisk, the 45-year-old White Sox catcher.

What should have been sweet — or bittersweet — has become all bitter.

Closing out his outstanding career, Fisk should be basking in the spotlight. Instead, he is feuding with management and sits ignored in a corner of the clubhouse.

The oblivion that Shakespeare described as "A great-sized monster of ingratitudes" is threatening Fisk. The word in Chicago is that as soon as he reaches Bob Boone's all-time record of 2,225 games caught, he will be gone.

I visited with Carlton in the White Sox clubhouse. He told me a story that might have foreboded his personal predicament.

It was after the sixth game of the 1975 World Series. Fisk's dramatic, 12th-inning home run had beaten the Reds. You've all seen the TV replay — Fisk, jumping along the first-base line with outstretched arms, coaxing the ball to stay fair. Fisk was the Hero of the World.

"What excitement," he recalled. "There was all kinds of attention. The press — radio and TV — kept me up late at the park. I finally had to pull away. My family was waiting.

"It was strange, but I had no place to spend the

night. I had been renting a house in Belmont, Mass., but the lease expired at the end of the season. We expected to get a hotel for the family.

"I got in the car, and I packed in my wife and two kids. We drove all over Boston looking for a hotel vacancy. Finally, the only solution was to drive 2½ hours to our home in New Hampshire and spend the night there. It was almost daylight by the time we got there.

"After a short and restless night, I drove back to Fenway for the final game of the Series. Needless to say, I was not too alert for the seventh game."

Ironic, isn't it, that after that historic home run, Fisk couldn't find a place to spend the night.

Once again, Carlton Fisk is having a difficult time finding a place to rest. Certainly, baseball history owes his heroism more than this.

Originally printed on June 11, 1993

Brave figured on new world

Jonh Smoltz was destined to be a Tiger. His grandfather worked on the Tiger Stadium grounds crew. And as a Lansing sandlotter, John dreamed of the day when he would pitch for the Tigers.

He signed with Detroit on Sept. 22, 1985, and began to pursue that dream. Then came the shock of his baseball life on Aug. 12, 1987.

"I was in the dugout at Glens Falls," he recalled. "Somebody handed me two notes. One said, 'Urgent. Call your father.' The other said to call Tiger Stadium."

John called his dad first.

"Have you heard?" his father asked.

"No, what?"

"You've been traded to Atlanta. I saw it on the news."

"I couldn't believe it," John said. "My dream of pitching for the Tigers was over. I called Tiger Stadium and Dave Miller confirmed the trade. Detroit was swapping me for Doyle Alexander. The Braves wanted me to report immediately to Richmond."

It was a good break for Smoltz. He had been struggling at Double-A Glens Falls, N.Y., at 4-10 and couldn't find himself.

"Detroit had only one roving pitching coach in the

whole organization," John said. "Our team would see him only twice a year. I was confused and needed help. The Braves sent me to the Instructional League. They had three pitching coaches there working with me one-on-one. The Tigers had always concentrated on my mechanics. The Atlanta coaches, especially Leo Mazzone, downplayed mechanics and zeroed in on perfecting my various pitches. They taught me to relax."

Smoltz had a great 1988 season at Triple-A Richmond, Va. He was 10-5 when he was called up. At 21, he was now a big-leaguer, but not with his dream team.

Since he was 7, Smoltz had loved the Tigers. He heard all their games on the radio. His dad and brothers would drive from Lansing to see the Tigers. His grandfather would interrupt his grounds crew duty, grab John by the hand, and introduce him to team executives Bill Lajoie and Jim Campbell.

"Someday," his grandfather would say, "this young man will be pitching for you guys."

Campbell and Lajoie had heard that boast from many relatives about many youngsters, but this time it almost came true.

Smoltz was an outstanding pitcher at Waverly High in Lansing. He starred in the Stan Musial League and the Junior Olympics. Yet most big-league clubs bypassed him.

"They were scared off by my decision to enroll at Michigan State," Smoltz said. "I already registered, but decided not to go at the last minute."

He was a Tiger for three years until the Alexander trade. Then he became a star with Atlanta.

But he will never forget Aug. 12, 1987, and the trade that changed the career of a young pitcher who had been destined to be a Tiger.

Originally printed on Sept. 11, 1992

Ernie Harwell

Puckett performed
like few others

Like anybody who follows baseball, I have a favorite major-leaguer. He is Kirby Puckett, centerfielder for the Minnesota Twins.

He's an animated bowling ball who performs with a verve and spirit that you see in few modern players.

It is evident to everybody that Puckett loves the game. And he is undoubtedly one of the major leagues' most exciting and appreciated players.

But if it hadn't been for the baseball strike in 1981, Puckett might never have become a big-leaguer. Jim Rantz was the Twins' assistant farm director then. He went to Illinois to watch his son play in a college game. But it was the performance of Puckett, on the opposing team, that caught Jim's eye.

Rantz returned to Minneapolis and told George Brophy, the team's farm director, what he had seen. On the strength of Rantz's recommendation, the Twins made Puckett their No. 1 draft choice in January 1982.

Puckett became a professional success in a hurry. In his first season, 1982, he played at Elizabethton, Tenn., and led the league in hitting with a .382 average. The next year, at Visalia, Calif., he batted .314. Each year he made the all-star team and each year he stole more than 40 bases. The Twins moved him to Toledo in 1984, but he didn't stay there long.

23

After 21 games with the Mud Hens, he was summoned by the Twins in Anaheim for a May 8 game against the Angels. Puckett's plane landed late at Los Angeles International Airport.

"I didn't know anything about L.A. or where Anaheim was," Puckett recalled. "So I told the cabbie to take me to the ballpark in Anaheim. The tab was $85, and I didn't have anywhere near that much money in my pocket. I told the cabbie to wait and went into the clubhouse, borrowed the money and took it to him."

The experience didn't seem to unnerve Puckett at all. In his debut, he went 4-for-5, stole a base and scored a run.

Between that smash debut and his 1991 playoff and World Series heroics, Puckett steadily built an outstanding career. He was the most valuable player in the '91 American League playoffs.

His performance in the sixth game of the World Series against Atlanta was classic. He made a sensational catch to rob Ron Gant of an extra-base hit and went 3-for-4 — a single, triple and home run. His homer off Charlie Leibrandt gave the Twins an 11th-inning victory.

Puckett entered the '92 season with a .320 lifetime batting average, third in the majors behind Wade Boggs (.345) and Tony Gwynn (.328). He won Gold Gloves in 1986-89 and in '91.

In his first year with the Twins, Puckett didn't hit a home run. In his second, he hit only four. Thanks to advice from Tony Oliva, he began to hit with power and consistency. Oliva taught Puckett how to keep his weight back and drive the ball.

Puckett is an all-around, genuine major league star. Baseball brought Kirby out of the ghetto in Chicago, and he has repaid the game with outstanding ability and true dedication. No wonder he's one of my favorites.

Originally printed on April 17, 1992

Detroit Free Press file photo

Big-league success didn't come instantly for Frank Tanana, who hurt his arm his senior season at Catholic Central High. But he persevered and went on to pitch for the Tigers.

Tanana was no sore loser

In a hot Midwestern summer in 1971, Frank Tanana was an overrated, overpaid, lonely rookie with a sore arm.

Frank almost didn't make it through that miserable season at Idaho Falls.

As a youngster in Detroit, he had dreamed of pitching for the Tigers. He was an outstanding schoolboy left-hander, and big-league scouts put him at the top of their lists. However, he hurt his arm while pitching for Catholic Central in his senior season.

"I tried to throw sidearm without being properly warmed up," Frank recalls. "Something popped. I began to favor that arm and got tendinitis in my left shoulder."

He kept trying to pitch. He even pitched in the Catholic finals in Detroit against Holy Redeemer. His arm hurt so much, he had to leave the game after four innings.

Tigers scouts and others sighed and scratched Tanana off their lists. But one scout — Carl Ackerman of the California Angels — stood firm. Ackerman had seen the young phenom fan 32 in a regional tournament at Cincinnati. On his recommendation, California made Tanana its first draft pick and gave him a $50,000 bonus.

Frank reported to Idaho Falls to begin his career — with a sore arm.

"I can't pitch. I have a bad arm," he told manager

Bob Clear. Clear shook his head, wondering what to do with a 17-year-old rookie pitcher who couldn't pitch.

When the bad news reached Anaheim, the Angels dispatched Ackerman to Idaho Falls to determine whether this sore-armed lefty was the same sensation he had signed. Ackerman urged the Angels not to give up on his prize prospect. Tanana went to California, where Dr. Frank Jobe examined him and told him the only cure would be complete rest for his ailing arm.

Frank was miserable. He had rejected a Duke basketball scholarship and now his baseball career appeared to be over before it had even begun.

He appeared in one game that season — as a pinch-runner.

His teammates resented him. On long bus trips, the $50,000 wonder was an easy target. "He's useless." "He's replacing somebody who could help us." "We don't need him."

Such abuse was so scathing on one trip that team leader Darrell Darrow intervened.

"Lay off the kid!" he shouted. "It's not Frank's fault. Someday his arm won't be sore and he'll be a big-leaguer. Give him a chance."

From then on, Tanana's rookie season was bearable. After a winter of rest, the arm recovered and Frank began his march to the majors.

After that miserable first year, he became a true big-league pitching star.

Originally printed on April 27, 1991

Time Machine

Doyle comes through in — and with — a pinch

The word came from baseball and is part of our language. It's "pinch-hit." The dictionary definition is: "To act as a substitute in an emergency."

There was a time back in the misty part of baseball when a pinch-hitter was a pinch-hitter in another sense of the word — an even truer sense, if you please.

It happened in 1914 and involved two of the most colorful figures in baseball history — John McGraw, the New York Giants manager, and famed umpire Bill Klem, who used to say: "I never miss one." This time, the pinch-hitter, Larry Doyle of the Giants, knew the old ump was wrong.

The Giants that year had a chance to beat out the Boston Braves for the National League pennant. Doyle strode to the plate in the ninth inning of a game at the Polo Grounds.

"Get on, Larry, any way you can!" McGraw shouted from the dugout. The pitcher wound up and fired a fastball. It ticked Doyle's bat. Larry started for first.

"Where do you think you're going?" Klem roared. "Come back here!" Doyle, already at first, refused to budge. "It hit your bat," Klem ruled. "It's a foul ball. Come back here and hit again."

Doyle started for the batter's box. As he did,

McGraw left the third base coach's box and met his player.

"Did the pitch hit you, Larry?" he asked.

"No, it didn't," Doyle answered.

"Then pinch yourself," the manager commanded. Doyle pinched himself while his manager stormed all over the umpire.

"It was a foul ball," Klem yelled at McGraw and Doyle.

"But Bill, it hit me before it hit the bat!" Doyle shouted. As McGraw diverted Klem's attention, Doyle gave himself a final, vicious pinch.

"Open your shirt," McGraw ordered. "Pull up your sweatshirt."

Klem took a look. Sure enough, he saw a welt where Doyle had come through in the pinch (or with the pinch).

"Take your base," Klem muttered reluctantly.

So that's how Larry Doyle became a pinch-hitter in the true sense of the word. And in the process, proved Klem wrong for the only time in his storied career.

Originally printed on Sept. 22, 2000

Pipp myths were as large as his famous headache

The height of fame is to have your name become a part of the language. Wally Pipp is that famous.

To do a "Wally Pipp" is for someone to take your job away because you didn't come to work.

All baseball fans know about Wally. A headache kept him out of a game in 1925, and Lou Gehrig replaced him at first base for the Yankees. Wally never got his job back.

In 1961, my wife and I visited Wally Pipp and his wife in Lansing. Spending the whole day together, we enjoyed our lunch and got in a lot of baseball talk. I was writing a piece on Wally for the Sporting News. He gave me a lot of background about himself and Gehrig — information I'd never heard before.

The common myth is that Gehrig started his consecutive-games streak on the day he substituted for Pipp. That's not true. Gehrig had pinch-hit the day before for Pee Wee Wanninger, the Yankees' shortstop. The next afternoon, Wally suffered his famous headache, and Gehrig replaced him.

Did you know that Pipp started his big-league career in 1913 with the Tigers? He hit a meager .161 in 12 games, so the Tigers shipped him to the minors. Two years later, Tigers owner Frank Navin sold Pipp to the Yankees.

Wally won the first base job and in 1916 became

the first Yankee to lead the league in homers (12). He won the home run title again the next season (nine). A fierce competitor, Wally had a fight with a teammate who also was a home run hitter — Babe Ruth.

"That was in 1922," Pipp recalled. "The Babe criticized the way I played first base, and I jumped him."

Pipp told me that he and the other Yankees thought Gehrig would never make the big leagues. That Yanks even offered Gehrig to the St. Louis Browns in a trade. Pipp scouted Gehrig when he played at Columbia. It was the first time he saw the big slugger. Their paths crossed again in September 1923. Pipp suffered a sprained ankle, and the Yankees recalled Gehrig from Hartford to replace Wally at first for the final week of the season.

Next came the famous headache. Somehow the story got out that Wally had been beaned in batting practice the day before he took his two aspirin and let Gehrig replace him. Not so, according to Pipp.

"I was beaned, all right," he said. "But it was a month after Lou took my place. Charlie Caldwell, a rookie pitcher, hit me in batting practice."

The next Pipp-Gehrig linkage came in Detroit in 1939. Pipp met Lou that morning at the Book Cadillac Hotel. Gehrig told Wally that he wasn't feeling well and probably wouldn't play that afternoon. Sure enough, that was the end of Gehrig's famous streak.

Wally Pipp died in Grand Rapids in 1965. He had a solid, 15-year major league career. But history will remember him for his famous headache.

Originally printed on May 10, 2000

For brawls, nothing beats Furillo-Durocher in '53

After a recent fracas between the Tigers and White Sox, several players asked me if that was the worst baseball fight I had ever broadcast. "Yes," I told them, "the worst melee between two teams. But I've seen more vicious fights involving two or three individuals."

Let's go back to Sept. 6, 1953, at the Polo Grounds. The Brooklyn Dodgers were running away with the pennant. When they faced the hated Giants that afternoon, they had an 11-game lead and had beaten New York nine straight times. In the second inning, Roy Campanella hit a two-run homer off Ruben Gomez. Gomez's next pitch hit Carl Furillo on the hand. Carl trotted to first base.

Suddenly, Furillo bolted toward the Giants' dugout. He charged at Giants manager Leo Durocher and grabbed him around the neck, throwing him to the ground. A Giants player (I think it was Monte Irvin) stepped on Furillo's right hand, spiking the Dodgers outfielder. Umpires finally quieted everybody and ejected Durocher and Furillo from the game.

After the game a writer asked Furillo, "How can you be so foolish to go after Durocher and his players when they are in their own dugout?"

Furillo replied: "I kept telling you guys that I'd get Leo. He made his pitchers throw at me too often."

"But Carl, you had to know that those Giant guys would be ganging up on you. They had you completely outnumbered."

"Didn't worry me," Furillo answered. "I knew a lot of those Giant guys hate Leo just like I do."

Furillo came out of that melee with broken bones in his left hand and missed 22 games. However, his forced rest assured him of the National League batting title. He hit .344, two points better than the Cards' Red Schoendienst.

Though not 100 percent, Furillo appeared in all six games of the World Series against the Yankees. His .333 batting average helped, but it wasn't enough to beat them.

How much difference a healthy Furillo would have made, we will never know. We do know that Carl never backed down from anything or anybody — not even Leo Durocher.

Furillo's hatred for the feisty manager was shared by many. Umpires probably felt more animosity against Leo than even rival players did. After the Furillo incident, a writer asked Bill Engeln, who was umpiring at first base, "Why didn't one of the Giants tag Furillo with the ball when he left first base to charge Durocher?"

"Oh, they couldn't do that," Engeln answered, "because I had called time so Carl could go get the SOB."

Originally printed on May 5, 2000

Hanky-panky on the side throws marriage curve

This is a story of love, lies and marriage. The names have been changed to protect the not-so-innocent in this vignette from a simpler time.

Herman Barwick was a Tigers star. He made a hefty salary and lived comfortably with his wife, Marge, in a small central Florida town. Herman had been invited to the Major League Baseball Players' golf tournament in Miami. He wanted to go and enjoy the pro-am, the banquet, and the good times with his baseball friends. But he had a problem. He didn't want to take his wife. He preferred the weekend companionship of his girlfriend, Cindy.

"I've been invited to this golf tournament," he told his wife. "But they don't allow women, so I'll have to leave you here at home."

"That's OK," Marge told him. "You go ahead without me. I know you'll enjoy being with the guys."

Herman spun his Cadillac convertible over to Cindy's, and soon the two were riding toward Miami. This was a time before superhighways and interstates, so their route took them through numerous small Florida communities.

One such burg was having a large celebration. As part of the festive occasion, the city fathers had decided to arbitrarily designate a tourist as the town's 100,000th visitor.

Herman and Cindy were flagged down at the town's only stoplight. In front of newsreel cameras, town officials awarded them special prizes, commemorative of the symbolic 100,000th visitor. The officials recognized Herman, the famous Tiger, and assumed Cindy was his wife.

After the weekend in Miami with Cindy, Herman returned home to his unsuspecting wife. Things went smoothly for about a week.

Then came the explosion.

Wife Marge was playing bridge with other Tigers wives.

"Marge," one of the ladies said, "I think you should go to the movies this week. The newsreel will be of special interest to you."

Before the Tigers' season ended, the marriage of Marge and Herman did.

Originally printed on June 30, 1999

Jackie Robinson and the trade that wasn't

Detroiter Dick Littlefield is the only player ever traded for Jackie Robinson.

If the December 1956 trade had not been nullified, Dick would hold the major league record for pitching for the most clubs.

In all the hoopla surrounding the Jackie Robinson commemorative year, the abortive trade received little attention.

"I was very proud the Dodgers thought enough of me to accept me in a trade for Robinson," Littlefield told me from his home in Detroit. "I'm sorry it didn't work out. I would have loved to have been a Brooklyn Dodger."

Why would the Dodgers want to trade Robinson, their superstar, to their hated rivals, the New York Giants?

I phoned Buzzie Bavasi, retired in his home in La Jolla, Calif. Buzzie was the Dodgers' general manager who made the deal.

"Jackie and our manager, Walt Alston, didn't get along," Bavasi said. "They had a personal confrontation during spring training of 1956 in Miami. That incident told me that Jackie didn't want to play for us anymore. So after the '56 season, I felt I could make a deal. Because I believed Jackie would agree to go only to a team in the New York area, I picked the Giants.

"I liked Dick Littlefield. He was a good, hard-nosed veteran pitcher. So I made the agreement with the Giants. They would give us Littlefield and $30,000 for Jackie. I called Robinson and told him about the deal. He had no comment for me. He voiced no objection to the trade and said nothing about retirement. We announced the deal Dec. 13, 1956. Two days later Look magazine hit the stands with an article by Jackie (as told to Tim Cohane) that he was retiring."

The Robinson-for-Littlefield trade was off. With his retirement, Jackie canceled the deal. Jackie was 37, and his knees ached. He took $50,000 from the editor of Look for his retirement article, and Littlefield stayed with the Giants.

Officially, Littlefield pitched for nine teams — but the number should be 10.

The Elias Sports Bureau, the official major league statistician, has ruled that two of Dick's teams (the St. Louis Browns and Baltimore Orioles) are counted as one. In their press guide, the Orioles maintain an independence from the Browns. But Elias is unmoved by that stance.

To me, Littlefield should share the record of pitching for 10 clubs with Robert L. Miller and Ken Brett. Also, those two pitched in expansion times. So they were with 10 teams out of 24. Dick was with 10 of 16. And, if the Robinson trade had not been canceled by Jackie's retirement, Littlefield would have pitched for 11 teams and held the all-time record.

Originally printed on Aug. 29, 1997

Mercer never did
win as a manager

Win Mercer didn't live up to his name; he never won a game as Tigers manager. In fact, he never actually managed the team. Yet, he should be listed as Tigers manager in 1903.

Mercer's story is one of the saddest in club history.

At the end of the 19th Century, he was the ace right-hander for Washington in the National League. Only 5-feet-7, he weighed 140 pounds. In 1896, he won 25 games for Washington. A career .286 hitter, he often played infield or outfield.

Mercer came to the Tigers in 1902. Pitching for a team that finished 52-83, he was 15-18 and had a career-best 3.04 ERA.

Owner Sam Angus decided to move Win's manager, Frank Dwyer, into the front office. He then selected the 28-year-old Mercer to manage the Tigers in 1903. The appointment of the handsome pitching star as manager met with fan approval, and Mercer's.

In the winter of 1902-03, the famous slugger of the 1880s, Tip O'Neill, took a team of American and National League All-Stars to California for an exhibition tour. Mercer went along to pitch and help O'Neill with the money. Mercer gambled and suffered huge losses; he became desperate.

On Jan. 12, 1903, Win Mercer committed suicide

in a room at the Oriental Hotel in San Francisco. He left O'Neill a letter, saying his financial accounts for the tour were in good order. He also wrote to his mother and his fiancee, both in Liverpool, Ohio. In the note to his mother, he apologized for the drinking and womanizing that led to his downfall.

Mystery still surrounds the death of Mercer, who had suffered from tuberculosis. The accounts say he asphyxiated himself, but they don't tell us exactly how.

His managerial career ended before it began. Mercer never has been officially listed as Tigers manager, but for two months in the off-season, the job was his.

Originally printed on June 8, 1996

AL's Ferrell caught all of the first Stars game

Rick Ferrell was the most surprised man at Comiskey Park when manager Connie Mack told him he was the American League's catcher in the first All-Star Game that warm July afternoon in 1933.

"I thought surely Mr. Mack would use Bill Dickey of the Yankees," Ferrell recalled in 1995, less than a month before his death at age 89.

"After all, Dickey was the Yankee batterymate of Lefty Gomez, the starting pitcher. When Connie came up to me and said, 'You're catching today,' I almost fell off the bench."

Rick caught the whole game. Alvin Crowder relieved Gomez in the fourth inning, yielding a homer to Frankie Frisch in the sixth. Lefty Grove took over in the seventh and blanked the Nationals the rest of the way.

Babe Ruth hit a two-run homer in the third for the American League, which won, 4-2.

"I thought Grove pitched the best for our side," Ferrell said. "But none of our pitchers had any trouble."

Compared to today's hoopla, there was very little ceremony connected to the game. The players arrived by train the night before and left as soon as the game was over.

"Connie Mack did have a pregame meeting the

morning of the game," Ferrell said. "He called us together at the Del Prado Hotel and talked to us. He said, 'You are all great ballplayers, but don't be upset if some of you don't get to play today. We came here to beat McGraw and those Nationals.' "

Mack and John McGraw had feuded since the early 1900s, and McGraw came out of retirement to manage the Nationals. Connie — more than anything — wanted to beat his rival and kept five of his 18 All-Stars (including Jimmie Foxx and Tony Lazzeri) on the bench. He kept a constant conversation with Ferrell between innings.

"I was surprised he was so alert at his age (70)," Ferrell said. "He kept asking me about the pitchers and waving his scorecard to position his defense. Once when I was at bat, he signaled for me to take a 3-1 pitch. I walked. Later on the bench he told me, 'Many times, a walk will upset the pitcher more than a hit.' "

The owners were opposed to that first All-Star Game. But because of pressure from Arch Ward, its originator, and added pressure from Ward's powerful paper, the Chicago Tribune, the game was staged as part of the 1933 World's Fair in Chicago.

"The game had something to prove," Ferrell said, "and it turned out to be a real success. After such a great reaction, the owners had to go along with it."

Ferrell couldn't remember the prize each player received for appearing in that first All-Star Game. It did not compare with some of the six-figure bonuses of today.

"It seems to me we got a ring," Ferrell said. "I

think it was worth about $25."

Ferrell had only his modest memento from that game, but he had his memories. He always will be the man who caught the entire first All-Star Game for the American League.

Originally printed on July 7, 1995

Berg did everything, except hit

For a lifetime .243 hitter, Moe Berg drew a lot of attention. He died in 1972, but they are still talking about Mysterious Moe and writing books about him.

Berg caught for five teams in the majors, averaging only 44 games a season. He was considered a smooth receiver who called a smart game.

In fact, to say he was smart was as much an understatement as saying Marie Antoinette died of a sore throat. The classic statement about Moe was: "He could speak a dozen languages but couldn't hit in any of them."

Berg was out of the majors before I got there, but I remember him as a scout in his post-playing days. He was a great conversationalist and always drew a crowd in any press room. Moe either had a lot of midnight blue suits or wore the same one all the time. I can't remember seeing him dressed any other way. He was a constant reader and loved newspapers but had a quirk: He would not read a paper if somebody else had read it first. His papers had to be virginal.

Berg graduated from Princeton magna cum laude and was offered a seat on the faculty. He turned down that offer to become a rookie shortstop with the Brooklyn Dodgers in 1923. In the off-season he attended the Sorbonne in Paris, studying experimental phonetics. Later, Moe graduated second in a class of 1,000 from Columbia Law School and was a successful attorney in the off-season.

Moe switched from the infield to catcher early in his career. Because he was a poor hitter, he spent most of his time in the bullpen, spinning yarns that entranced his teammates.

Once during Joe Cronin's reign as Red Sox manager, one of his pitchers was late answering Joe's summons from the bullpen. When the pitcher reached the mound, Joe asked, "Why are you late? Where you been?"

"Sorry, Joe," answered the pitcher. "I had to wait till Moe Berg finished his story."

But Berg's real fame came as a spy. In 1934 while on an All-Star tour of Japan, Moe took photos that were used during the planning of Gen. Jimmy Doolittle's 1942 raids over Tokyo. During World War II, Berg was sent on secret missions to Norway, Yugoslavia and Germany. He also went to Italy to arrange passage to America for nuclear scientists.

His most fantastic adventure was tracking down Werner Heisenberg, Germany's No. 1 atomic scientist. The scientist told Moe that Germany's nuclear research was lagging behind that of the Allies.

When President Franklin D. Roosevelt was told of Berg's report, he said, "Let's pray Heisenberg is correct. And my regards to the catcher."

Around the press rooms, Berg never spoke of his days as a spy. He was all baseball. You would see him every year at the World Series, and he loved to talk about the game.

When Moe died in a New Jersey hospital, his final words were, "How'd the Mets do today?"

He was baseball's smartest man. But he couldn't hit a curveball.

Originally printed on July 14, 1995

Old-timer was a lefty-hating King

I n the 1940s, I hung around a lot of minor league players and heard a lot of stories. Some might even have been true.

Whenever the veterans gathered, somebody would start talking about John King, an old-timer who violently hated left-handed pitchers. King's legend gained credibility when Collie Small wrote an article about him in Colliers magazine. I still remember some of those stories.

John King was a top-notch player. He led several leagues in stolen bases, had a great throwing arm and could hit — at least, until he had to face a left-hander. They baffled him, and his inability to solve them brought out his hatred for anybody left-handed.

King was walking down the street when he passed a blind beggar with a violin and dropped a quarter into the beggar's cap. In gratitude, the beggar began to play a lively tune for King.

Suddenly, King wheeled around. The beggar was playing his violin left-handed.

"Dammit," King told himself, "I can't get away from these left-handers." He reached into the beggar's cap and took back his quarter.

One afternoon a small boy was trying to climb over the fence onto the baseball field. He was having trouble and he called to King, playing in the outfield, to help him. King went to the youngster and pulled him over the fence. But the boy made a big mistake. He picked up a pebble and threw it — with his left hand. An angry King whirled on him, picked him up and threw him back over the fence.

King often would punish himself because of the humiliation left-handers inflicted on him. One hot Texas afternoon when he was playing for Longview, a left-hander struck him out in a crucial at-bat. John was disgusted with himself. He broke his bat over the dugout steps, went to the water pail and drew a dipper of water. He held the dipper high and in a mock toast to himself shouted so all in the ballpark could hear.

"John King, you'd like a drink of water, wouldn't you? Your jaws are dry. There's cotton on your tongue, and your taste buds need a sprinkle. But, dang your worthless hide. You're not getting any water. You won't get one swallow till you go out there and get a hit off that varmint of a left-hander."

In those more informal times, King confessed that he often spat in the face of a left-handed pitcher. If he were on third base, he would fill his mouth with water. While the pitcher was winding up, John would race to the mound and spit water in his face. He then would run back to third while the pitcher completed his windup and threw to the plate.

King's baseball's career was interrupted by World War I. He went to France and was there when the war ended. When he came home, he was still protesting against left-handers.

"Fifty thousand left-handed soldiers went to

France," he moaned, "and all 50,000 came back without a scratch. There is no justice."

When King's playing career ended, he became an umpire. But he discovered oil on his West Texas land and gave up baseball.

He never lost his hatred for left-handers, though. When his only son was born, he was fearful the baby might grow up to be a left-hander. He was shocked to see the child reach for his rattle with his left hand.

Desperately, he stuffed the baby's left hand into a tobacco sack, tying the drawstring around the baby's wrist. His son's hand stayed tied until King was sure that his baby wasn't going to be a left-hander after all.

Originally printed on June 16, 1995

'27 Yanks were the best, but not at the bank

Baseball strike talk always brings up conversation about salaries. The average fan cannot comprehend the high salaries of today and is jealous.

There was no such problem in 1927. That year's New York Yankees are considered by most to be baseball's greatest team. And though those players made more money than the average worker, their payroll would not be enough for a star's tip money today.

The Yankees' superstar was Babe Ruth, and the Babe was paid accordingly. In fact, his yearly salary was greater than the rest of the starting lineup.

Babe made $70,000 in 1927. His teammates' salaries were: Benny Bengough, catcher, $8,000; Lou Gehrig, first base, $8,000; Tony Lazzeri, second base, $8,000; Mark Koenig, shortstop, $7,000; Joe Dugan, third base, $12,000; Bob Meusel, leftfield, $12,000; Earle Combs, centerfield, $10,500.

So, besides Ruth, the Yankees' starting lineup totaled $65,500, or $4,500 less than the Babe.

Herb Pennock led the pitchers with a salary of $17,500; the others were paid from $2,500 to $13,000. Reserve infielders and outfielders made from $1,800 to $7,000.

I found it interesting that the outfielders' salaries were higher than the infielders' — despite the fact the Yankees had some great stars in the infield. Granted, Gehrig was in the early years of his career, but he was already a superstar. In 1927, he batted .373, hit 47 home runs and led the American League in RBIs with 175 — all for $8,000.

Dugan, the highest-paid infielder, was in his 11th year of a 14-year major league career and was regarded as one the game's top third basemen. Two footnotes about Joe: (1) When the Red Sox traded him to New York in July during the heated 1922 pennant race, there was so much controversy about the trade that the uproar brought about a June 15 trading deadline the following year. (2) Dugan ended his career with the Tigers in 1931. He appeared in only eight games and had four singles in 17 at-bats.

Getting back to the Yankees' payroll, I figure that in 1927 the entire team was paid less than $170,000. In '94, the average big-league salary was $1,200,000.

The 1927 Yankees might have been the greatest, but they won't rank high in the salary history of the sport.

Originally printed on Sept. 9, 1994

Crackers crumbled in playoff idea

While everybody is trying to figure out whether the new playoff system next year will work in the major leagues, this is an anniversary year for playoffs.

They started in the minors in 1933 and were the brainchild of Frank Shaughnessy, business manager of the Montreal Royals.

Shaughnessy derived the idea from hockey and convinced the International League to use his plan. It was a success, providing interest in the final weeks of the season and a boost in attendance. Other leagues followed the Shaughnessy plan, and it now is a part of baseball history.

However, the lower minors had used various gimmicks to save a runaway season even before that. One of those ideas, contrived by the Southern League, ruined my boyhood summer of 1928.

I was 10 and had been following my hometown heroes, the Atlanta Crackers, for two seasons. The Crackers didn't play well in the first few months of 1928. The Birmingham Barons, their hated rivals, had raced to a large lead by mid-season.

In their combined wisdom, league owners voted to split the season. They sensed a runaway for the Barons and a large drop in attendance. (This splitting of the season was nothing new in the minors.) Now it was established that the teams would begin a new season in July, and the second-half winner would battle the Barons for the pennant in a playoff.

My team, the Crackers, began to roll. They took the league lead, and it seemed certain that they would win the second half and meet Birmingham for the championship. One Saturday night, I went to bed happy because my Crackers were on top.

The next morning, I was shocked by headlines telling me that the Crackers dropped into last place.

It seems that the hated Barons blew the whistle on the Crackers. The Southern League rules stated that each team could have only so many "A" players (players with certain experience) on their rosters. The Crackers had been using too many "A" players in their drive to first place.

So the league ruled that 14 Crackers victories be turned into losses. That dropped the Crackers all the way to eighth place.

My most vivid memory of that summer of 1928 is opening the sports section on that certain Sunday morning to find that my heroes no longer were leading the league. It was the greatest shock I've ever experienced as a baseball fan.

It made my summer a bummer.

Originally printed on Sept. 17, 1993

Appling's still a Sox symbol

Chicago is excited about baseball. The old town should be excited. People are talking about an all-Chicago World Series. The Cubs keep on celebrating their old ballpark, and the White Sox are starting to celebrate their new one.

An outstanding shortstop historically symbolizes each of these teams. The Cubs on the north side salute Ernie Banks; the south side White Sox look to Luke Appling. Banks, retired for many years, still beams, "Let's play two." Luke died early in 1991 but remains the consummate White Sox star.

Most people remember Luke as the champion at fouling off pitches until he got a good one. Some recall him as the outstanding Sick Man of Baseball. I wrote an article about Luke for Sport magazine in 1948 and titled it "The Sick Man of Baseball." The whole point of the piece was that the worse Luke felt, the better he played. He always was moaning about his health. Nobody resented that because they all knew Luke didn't mean it. He would moan, but he still had that happy, pixie grin that told all of us how much he enjoyed baseball and life in general.

Appling was one of my boyhood heroes. He grew up in Atlanta, my hometown. My first memory of Luke goes back to 1930, when he hit four homers for his Oglethorpe College team.

After college, he immediately signed with the Atlanta Crackers. He hit .326 that first year, and Crackers owner Rell J. Spiller sold him to the White

Sox. Strangely enough, Luke almost became a Cub. Spiller thought he had a deal with Cubs president Bill Veeck Sr. He even wired Luke (on a trip with the Crackers to Little Rock, Ark.) that the Cubs had acquired him.

But the transaction fell through. Spiller then contacted the White Sox. Chicago sent Atlanta $20,000, plus an outfielder, Poco Taitt, to complete the transaction.

Luke lasted 20 years, all with the White Sox. In 1964, he was selected to the Hall of Fame. In 1982, he gained a new notoriety when at 75 he banged a home run in the Crackerjack Old-Timers game in Washington off 61-year-old Warren Spahn.

The story that best characterized "Old Aches and Pains" happened early in his career. Luke built a fine home on the outskirts of Atlanta. The centerpiece of the Appling estate was a lake where Luke loved to fish. When the Applings were in Chicago for the summer, the neighborhood kids often disregarded Luke's "No Fishing" sign. The caretaker wired Appling and asked: "Is it all right for the kids to fish in your lake?"

Appling wired back. "OK for kids to fish in lake. Don't let them know I said so. It might spoil their fun."

The happy moaner Luke Appling was a great friend and companion. Like Banks is to the Cubs, Luke is the symbol of White Sox history.

Originally printed on April 20, 1991

They Changed
the Game

Ernie Harwell Collection

Lulu and I have been married for almost 60 years. The 1999 season marked a first for us: Lulu watched a Tigers game with me from the broadcast booth.

Ernie Harwell Collection

The only time I did not work in radio or television was the four years I served during World War II.

Commissioner Landis wasn't the friendliest man

This is about my meeting with baseball's first commissioner, Kenesaw Mountain Landis.

It was October 1943. America was at war and I was back home in Atlanta — on leave from the U.S. Marines.

"I'm going to the World Series in New York," I told my wife, Lulu. "I'll hitch a ride on a Navy transport. If I can't get a flight, I'll come back home."

I hitched a ride as far as Washington, arriving there about midnight. I took a train to New York, standing up all the way in a crowded, smelly coach.

This was my first trip to New York, and as I came out of Penn Station the size of the city overwhelmed me. I flagged a cab and asked the driver to take me to a place where a Marine could spend the night. He dumped me at Columbus Circle. An armory there had two or three thousand cots. Holding onto my wallet, I spent the night there.

Late the next morning I walked to the Commodore Hotel, where Commissioner Landis was staying for the World Series. I had no ticket and no idea about how to get one. Hanging around the lobby, I saw the commissioner coming by on the way to his limousine. He was flanked by his secretary and a couple of aides.

Landis was a gaunt, 76-year-old with flowing gray hair. He shuffled slowly through the crowded lobby.

I jumped right in front of the commissioner and his entourage.

"Hello, Commissioner," I said to him. "Do you have an extra ticket to the game this afternoon?"

He didn't break his shuffle. He looked at me in my uniform (wartime, remember, and we had to wear the uniform all the time). With a quick glance my way he said, "Hello, Marine." Then he continued his shuffle through the lobby.

That was my association with the first commissioner. Since then, I've known the other eight a lot better than I knew Judge Landis, who died Nov. 25, 1944.

Just a footnote. I did get to see that Series game. I took the subway to Yankee stadium. When I got to the end of a long line at the ticket window, several fans shouted, "Marine, go to the head of the line!" I did. I put down my $3.30 and bought a ticket in the upper deck.

Originally printed on Sept. 5, 1998

Cobb's 4,000th wasn't a hit in print

Remember all the hoopla surrounding Pete Rose's chase for his 4,000th hit?
I mention this because it's the 70th anniversary of Ty Cobb becoming the first player to collect 4,000 hits. The historic hit was hardly mentioned in the next morning's Detroit Free Press.

The hit came July 18, 1927. Cobb had returned to Navin Field as a member of the Philadelphia Athletics. He doubled off Sam Gibson in the first inning. The headline over the game story read: "First Inning Rally Wins for Bengals over Lefty Grove."

The first subhead said: "Fothergill's home run accounts for two scores as Tigers count three times and wipe out rival team's lead." Cobb was still ignored in the second subhead, "Gibson holds Athletics in check after opening frame — Heilmann features Detroit attack with quartet of safeties."

Even the story's lead ignored Cobb's hit. After four long paragraphs he got a mention, but an oblique one. Writer Harry Bullion put it this way: "Gibson stopped Simmons cold and he was effective against Cobb after the first inning when a lucky double slid off Heilmann's gloved hand and helped in the making of two runs."

That's all the coverage the historic No. 4,000 got in the game story.

The Free Press ran a column of notes, with the headline: "Bengals in third place; Ty Cobb gets 4,000th hit."

But the note on the hit came in the fifth paragraph, after Bullion had listed the upcoming schedule and that the Tigers didn't make a double play. Then he mentioned the hit: "When Cobb made his fluke double in the first inning, it was his 4,000th major league safety. He's so far ahead of all records of other batsmen that he will never be beaten or tied."

There was no photo of Cobb, no stats or other mention of his hit.

The Detroit News didn't give Cobb's hit any more attention. It did mention the feat in the headline — the same size head accorded the Detroit team that won the YMCA world basketball title. H.G. Salsinger wrote the game story and passed off the event with one sentence.

He wrote: "Cobb hit a line drive into rightfield and Heilmann, trying for a one-handed catch, got his glove on the ball but it bounced out and gave Cobb a scratch two-bagger."

Salsinger wrote a column that afternoon but devoted all of it to boxing's lightweight division.

The News had no story on the historic double or any photo.

There's no doubt sports coverage has changed in the past 70 years.

Originally printed on July 18, 1997

Ernie Harwell Collection

Together with Red Sox slugger Ted Williams. In 1997, Williams led a charge to get Shoeless Joe Jackson of the White Sox elected to the Hall of Fame.

Going to bat for Shoeless Joe

Ted Williams went to bat for Shoeless Joe Jackson.
The famed Boston Red Sox slugger supported a drive to elect the disgraced outfielder to the Hall of Fame.

Although many efforts have been made to clear Jackson of his involvement in the infamous Black Sox scandal of 1919, none has succeeded.

Jackson was a career .356 hitter for the Athletics, Indians and White Sox in 1908-20.

"I've put a great deal of study into the issue," said Williams, elected to the Hall in 1966. "And I truly believe that Jackson belongs in the Baseball Hall of Fame. He was an outstanding and dominant player of his era. While alive, he served his 60-year sentence of being banned from the game. I think his suspension should be lifted. After that maybe we can get him into the Hall of Fame."

In 1997, Williams met with board members of the Society for American Baseball Research to present his views. The research group agreed to provide Ted more background on Jackson and to discuss his proposal at its convention in Louisville, Ky., that summer.

Williams also wanted to enlist former players and media to support his drive for Jackson.

I served six years with Williams on the Hall of Fame veterans committee. From my personal experience I know he is very thorough and dedicated.

Also, he is an open and forthright advocate once he believes in a cause. Certainly, Jackson could have no better supporter because Williams has tremendous prestige and respect among baseball people.

"I became interested in Jackson's case after seeing the film 'Eight Men Out,'" Williams said. "I began to read all the books and articles about his banishment from baseball. Sure, he took the money, but he tried to return it and Harry Grabiner, the White Sox official, told him to keep it."

From his early playing days, Williams heard constant praise of Jackson's hitting prowess.

"Ty Cobb told me that Jackson was baseball's greatest natural hitter," Williams said. "Also, Babe Ruth said he copied his swing from Jackson."

As a rookie, Williams learned more about Jackson from his teammate and manager, Joe Cronin, and from Red Sox executive Eddie Collins.

"Eddie was on that Black Sox team," Williams said. "He never discussed the game-throwing charges, but he did often tell me what a great hitter he thought Joe Jackson was."

Williams is convinced that Jackson, who died in 1951, should be exonerated. "Remember," Williams said, "he was never proven guilty in a court of law."

I'm sure Ted met some opposition in his support of Jackson. But he convinced me that his cause is right.

Originally printed on May 30, 1997

Jackie stole home and my imagination

The most significant event in professional sports history came when Jackie Robinson broke baseball's color line. His heroics not only changed the course of baseball, but brought the great black athletes into other sports.

In my personal corner of the world, Robinson looms large. His powerful presence proved a force in the first inning of my very first major league broadcast.

Still fighting all kinds of prejudice, Jackie was in the middle of his second season when I joined the Brooklyn Dodgers. Red Barber was ill, and Dodgers president Branch Rickey summoned me from Atlanta. I was scared and nervous — even more so when my first scheduled broadcast was delayed another agonizing 24 hours by a rainout.

It was a night game at Brooklyn's Ebbets Field on Aug. 4, 1948 — the Dodgers vs. the Cubs. The customers hardly had time to settle into their seats when, with two out in the first inning, Robinson danced off third and raced for home.

Cubs pitcher Russ Meyer fired the ball to catcher Bob Scheffing. Robinson slid. Umpire Frank Dascoli called him safe.

Waving his arms, Meyer charged the umpire. His profanities and obscenities crackled over our field microphone. Dascoli ejected him.

After Dutch McCall replaced Meyer, the Cubs rallied and took the lead in the fifth, 4-2. But the Dodgers tied the game in the eighth and won in the ninth when Bruce Edwards' two-out single scored Gene Hermanski from second.

What I best remember from that game is Robinson's steal of home, which was symbolic of the excitement he created throughout his career.

My next year with the Dodgers, I watched Robinson drive his team to a pennant. He led the National League in hitting with a .342 average and was named National League most valuable player.

Now it has come full circle. On April 5, 1997, the Dodgers saluted Robinson before their home game with Pittsburgh. His widow, Rachel, was there, along with his friends and former teammates.

I was there, too, broadcasting for CBS Radio. It was the first week of my 50th season in the big leagues. Yet, as long as I broadcast, I probably won't ever see a more stirring moment than when Robinson stole home in the first inning of my first game.

Originally printed on March 28, 1997

Two wins in a day . . . never again

His name appears every year in "On This Date." Otherwise, it seems as if nobody has heard of an Iowa farm-boy pitcher named Emil Levsen.

We'll see his name with the entry on Aug. 28, the day Levsen started, finished and won two games in one day.

That afternoon at Fenway Park, Dutch Levsen beat the Red Sox, 6-1 and 5-1. He allowed four hits in each game. The first game lasted one hour, 29 minutes; the second went 1:48. He became the 39th player to pitch two complete-game victories in one day. Nobody has done it since. He did it 75 years ago.

Some stars who have accomplished the feat are Carl Mays, Cy Young, Ed Walsh, Urban Shocker and Grover Cleveland Alexander. But the doubleheader king of the mound is Joe McGinnity. In August 1903, McGinnity pitched both ends of three doubleheaders and won all six games for the New York Giants.

When Levsen achieved his double victory, he was expecting to pitch only one game. However, he had such an easy time in the opener that he asked manager Tris Speaker if he could pitch the second game.

"I don't think you should," Speaker told him. "You might hurt your arm."

"Don't worry, I'll be all right," Levsen told his manager. Speaker relented. Levsen didn't even warm up for the second game.

Levsen's double win was the highlight of his 1926 season, his only decent year. He pitched six seasons — all with Cleveland, winning 21 and losing 26.

In 1950, Don Newcombe of the Brooklyn Dodgers became the last major leaguer to attempt Levsen's feat. Newcombe won an easy first game against the Phillies at Shibe Park.

"Hey, big guy, that was an easy one," manager Burt Shotton told Newcombe. "Why not pitch the second one, too?"

"OK, give me the ball," Newk answered. But Shotton thought his pitcher was kidding. Newcombe assured Burt he was serious, took a quick shower, got an arm rub and walked onto the field to warm up. He didn't win the second game that afternoon. He didn't even finish. Newcombe left that game with his team trailing, 2-1, after seven innings. Thanks to a Jackie Robinson home run, the Dodgers rallied and won, 3-2, for reliever Dan Bankhead.

Today, we'll never see a pitcher start, finish and win a doubleheader. Teams play only a few double-headers now and most managers don't even expect their starter to finish one game — and certainly not two.

Originally printed on Aug. 24, 1995

Ernie Harwell Collection

Joe DiMaggio's personality probably couldn't hold up in today's game, but his 56-game hitting streak will likely always stand.

DiMaggio's streak
is a record for all time

T he baseball record least likely to be broken is Johnny Vander Meer's feat of back-to-back no-hitters. I don't think any pitcher will ever throw three straight.

My next choice as the record never to be broken is Joe DiMaggio's 56-game hitting streak. Since DiMaggio set that mark in 1941, a few stars have taken shots at it. Pete Rose and Paul Molitor made runs, but both proved how difficult the record is to match.

Now in our day of high-hype media madness, busting the record becomes even tougher. In DiMag's time there was newspaper and radio coverage, and even though the streak enthralled baseball fans all over the country, Joe managed to keep his sanity.

He was a different star for a different time. DiMaggio was cool and aloof and protected well by those around him. In his day, the New York press was the single most powerful media arm. The baseball writers in New York accepted Joe's aloofness and built him into a classic icon. DiMaggio held court for his favorites at Toot Shor's restaurant and the writers repaid him with an homage accorded only the likes of Jack Dempsey, Red Grange, Bobby Jones or Babe Ruth.

Under the same circumstances today, the investigative nature of the media would have given DiMag much different treatment. He would have been severely criticized for his standoffishness, and his private life would have been shredded.

The 1941 season not only featured DiMaggio's famous streak, it was also the year Ted Williams batted .406. Just to emphasize the contrasting attitude of the media toward these two stars, the baseball writers that season gave the Most Valuable Player Award to DiMaggio.

Williams feuded with the press and had only a few friends among the writers. DiMaggio cultivated the most influential writers, who in turn convinced their peers that Joe was a classy guy who wanted to be left alone.

It's ironic that Williams, a truly outgoing person, was castigated by the press and DiMaggio, a cool recluse, was deified. Today, Ted is sort of a mellow senior statesman for the game and Joe (though still revered) became a baseball hermit, best known by later generations as Mr. Coffee, or one of Marilyn Monroe's husbands.

I've known Williams much better than I've known DiMaggio. Ted was always warm and friendly toward me during his playing career. In later days, we've become closer, serving on the veterans committee for the Baseball Hall of Fame.

I hardly knew DiMaggio when he played. I was working in the National League when Joe was finishing his career.

Later, I got to know him in his post-playing days. He was reserved when you first met him. But after he thought you had some real knowledge about him or baseball, he warmed up. He was friendly and direct in my interviews, and always polite.

In my most recent interview he told me about his cab ride to the Cleveland ballpark the night his streak was broken.

"I was riding along with Gomez," he said of pitcher Lefty Gomez. "The cabbie just had a feeling. He turned around and said, 'Joe, I just have a feeling that tonight is going to be the night that they're going to break your streak,' and Gomez jumped all over him and he kind of felt miserable about it because he told me later on, 'You know, that bothered me throughout the whole ballgame.'"

The streak was broken that night. Its ending did not bother DiMaggio too much. He went out and hit in the next 16 games.

Originally printed on April 26, 1995

Brock's cupped bat was oh-so-significant

Everybody at the 25th anniversary party for the 1968 Tigers and Cardinals wanted to ask Lou Brock about his World Series nonslide. I wanted to ask him about cupped bats, which he brought from Japan and introduced to the big leagues.

"After the 1968 World Series, I went with the Cardinals to Japan," he said. "I watched Sadaharu Oh hit some tremendous home runs. I asked him to give me one of his bats. He was kind enough to do it.

"The bat was different. It was cupped at the end of the barrel where the wood had been hollowed out."

"What's the theory behind this cupped bat?" I asked him.

"It's made that way," he said, "to take the weight from the end and give the bat true balance.

"I tried the new bat and liked it. The next year, I began to use the Oh bat in the National League. It worked well for me.

"There were some protests at first. But the bat was legal, as long as it was made from only one piece of wood.

"I had only a few models of the Oh bat and had a hard time keeping them. I'd be careful after a time at bat and always toss the bat to a batboy. Otherwise, someone would steal it.

"When I got my 3,000th hit, I was using the cupped bat. Now, I notice that between one-third and one-half of the big-leaguers use that kind of bat.

"The ironic twist about the cupped bat is that it originated in America," Brock said. "The Japanese copied it.

"Around 1910, the Savannah Bat Co. manufactured what was called the teacup model. It was similar to the cupped bat we have today. Nobody paid much attention to it. Somehow, years later the Japanese ran across the teacup and from it designed their own version.

"Who first came up with the teacup idea? I don't know, but since the Savannah Bat Co. was located in Georgia, I have a strong feeling it might have been Ty Cobb."

Originally printed on Aug. 27, 1993

Chadwick gave the game a gift

Where would baseball be without the box score?

It's the perfect condensation of a game. Nowhere in any other sport can we get such a succinct summary.

The man who gave us this little gem of the diamond was Henry Chadwick.

Chadwick came up with the idea of the box score in 1859.

As the baseball editor of the New York Clipper, he was covering a game in South Brooklyn between the Stars and the Excelsiors when he made his contribution to baseball record-keeping.

He adapted the box score from the scorecard he used in cricket, and he included the names of the players and details of their performances.

The box score has lasted all through the years.

Sure, there have been changes, but its basic form has remained. It is must reading every day for millions of fans all over the world.

The box score was only one of Chadwick's gifts to baseball. In 1858 he wrote the first rule book. Fifteen years later, he started the first baseball weekly, "The Ball Player's Chronicle."

In the 1870s, Chadwick led a successful crusade to rid baseball of gambling. In the 1880s, he published the first fan paper of the game — "The

Metropolitan," a journal of the polo grounders.

He became editor of the Spalding Baseball Guide in 1888 and held that job until his death in 1908.

Chadwick was awarded the Medal of Achievement at the World's Fair in 1904 and in 1938 was named by a special committee to the Baseball Hall of Fame.

Chadwick was born in England in 1824. He came to America when he was 13 years old.

His first writing job was covering cricket for the Long Island Star. It was at a cricket game in 1856 that he observed some boys playing baseball at the edge of the cricket field.

This new game enthralled him and he decided that baseball was the sport he wanted to cover. Chadwick became a one-man press association, writing for several New York papers and other eastern dailies.

He began elaborate record-keeping and became the game's first statistician. He covered baseball the rest of his life, and died at the age of 84.

His career reached into modern baseball, but it had its beginning with the very first club in baseball history, the Knickerbockers.

After Chadwick's death, a large monument was erected in tribute to him in Brooklyn's Greenwood Cemetery.

Chadwick was called the father of baseball. He gave the game many lasting gifts — and the greatest of these was the box score.

Originally printed on Sept. 4, 1992

Cobb helped Joe clip the Yanks' GM

Ty Cobb wasn't only a great player, he was a great negotiator at contract time. The Georgia Peach was just as tough when fighting for a higher salary as he was sliding, spikes high, into a base.

Ty's career was finished eight years before another baseball great, Joe DiMaggio, reached the big leagues. Yet Tyrus helped young Joe's negotiations with the Yankees' front office.

DiMaggio told me the story this way:

"After the Yankees bought my contract from the San Francisco Seals, Ed Barrow, their general manager, offered me $4,000 for my rookie season in 1936. I was just a raw kid and I had heard how tough Barrow was in negotiations, so I needed some help.

"I knew Ty Cobb slightly. But my brother Tom, who ran our restaurant, knew him even better. Cobb came into the restaurant often, and Tom either wouldn't charge him for his meal or he would let him have it at half-price. Of course, Ty was a millionaire several times over. But he still liked the idea of a free meal.

"Tom told Cobb about my contract offer, and Cobb invited Tom and me to his home in Palo Alto. He wrote out a letter to Barrow, saying the $4,000 was too low a salary. I copied the letter in my handwriting and signed my name.

"Barrow sent back a new contract. This time he was offering $4,500. I consulted with Cobb, and he said, 'Hold out for more.' So he wrote another letter. I copied it and signed my name. The Yankees came back with another offer, $5,000. That seemed like a lot of money to me, and I was ready to settle for it. Cobb said no, so we wrote another letter. This time Barrow went up another $500. We were now at $5,500. Cobb didn't think it was enough.

" 'You're worth more, son,' he told me. 'Don't give up now. Let's go at him again.'

"Cobb wrote another letter. Again I copied it, signed it and mailed it to Barrow. In 10 days, here came the answer. Barrow sent a contract for $6,000. He also enclosed a letter in which he told me that was his final offer. It was take or leave it.

"I showed the letter to Cobb. 'Take it, Joe,' he told me. 'You whipped Mr. Barrow. Now, go do it to the rest of the American League.'

"Barrow never knew that Cobb was my unofficial adviser. He knew that my brother Tom was acting as my agent and thought that all the negotiating was done by Tom and me. Along with that final letter, Barrow got a little more generous and sent a bonus.

"But the bonus wasn't for me. It was for my brother Tom — two new suits."

And that's how two baseball greats hooked up to outsmart one of baseball's craftiest general managers.

Originally printed on September 23, 1994

Innovations?
Got to hand it to Hawk

Long before colorful White Sox broadcaster Ken (Hawk) Harrelson began entertaining TV listeners, he was a charismatic and talented major league star. He was a key factor in Boston's pennant drive in 1967 and also played for Cleveland, Washington and Kansas City.

It was at K.C. in 1963 that the Hawk made his lasting contribution to baseball — introducing the now ubiquitous batting glove. At the time, it was a golf glove.

Nobody had ever used a golf glove — or any other kind of glove — while batting. New York Giants outfielder Bobby Thomson had worn one once in batting practice but never ventured into a game with it. Then, along came Harrelson.

"I had played 27 holes of golf that afternoon," he recalled. "My right hand had blistered, but that did not worry me because I knew I wouldn't play in the game that night against the Yankees since they were pitching a right-hander.

"When I got to the park, I found out that the Yanks weren't pitching a right-hander. Instead, they were using Whitey Ford. I found a golf glove in my locker and used it. I hit two home runs off Whitey.

"The next night against the Yanks, I wore the glove again. But so did Mickey Mantle, Roger Maris and a lot of other Yankee players."

In a few years, the golf glove became the batting glove. Its use is now universal — thanks to Harrelson's 27 holes of golf and his blistered hand.

Ken was also the player who popularized the sweatband (or wristband) in the big leagues.

Harrelson was one of those colorful players who was cool before it was cool to be cool. He was a pacesetter and thought it was cool to wear sweatbands when he was in the minor leagues.

"I took a lot of abuse for that," he said. "Guys got on me about it. They thought I was a hot dog, a showboat. But I sweat a lot, and the sweat would roll down my arms and bother me when I batted. The sweatbands were very helpful to me in dealing with that problem."

Now, many big leaguers wear the wristbands, which have become much larger and more sophisticated. Some players' wristbands are so large now that they extend all the way up to the elbow. Many have a club insignia or other logos on them. They've come a long way since the Hawk wore his in the minors.

Harrelson had a nine-year playing career. In 1968, he hit 35 homers for the Red Sox; he hit 30 in '69, split between the Red Sox and Indians.

He also has played on the pro golf tour and served as general manager of the White Sox. It's ironic that Harrelson's most lasting contribution to baseball was his introduction of two pieces of equipment — the batting glove and the wristband.

Originally printed on July 22, 1994

Nuxhall is red-faced no more

When he ran out of the Reds dugout in 1944, he fell flat on his face. Now Joe Nuxhall stands tall as one of the most beloved figures in Cincinnati sports history.

I was thrilled to watch the pregame celebration at Riverfront Stadium when the Reds and their fans honored Nuxhall, who endeared himself to Reds fans as an announcer.

On June 10, 1944, Nuxhall became the youngest player in a major league game. He was 15 years old.

Nuxhall allowed the St. Louis Cardinals five runs in two-thirds of an inning in relief. He didn't return to the majors until eight years later.

Nuxhall still holds the record as baseball's youngest. He recalled that day with a chuckle.

"I borrowed a friend's car to drive from my hometown, Hamilton, to Crosley Field," he said. "Of course I was underage, and a cop pulled me over for speeding. I was scared to death, and I never drove again until I got my license."

Manager Bill McKechnie told Joe to relax, sit on the bench and enjoy the game.

A week before, Nuxhall had been pitching to 14- and 15-year-old kids; now, he was in the big leagues during World War II. When the Cards battered their way to a 13-0 lead, McKechnie decided to test the rookie in the ninth inning.

"I grabbed my glove and headed for the bullpen," Joe recalled. "But I tripped on the top step and went sprawling. What a way to start in the big leagues!"

Nuxhall retired two of the first three hitters, but then the roof caved in. He surrendered five earned runs, and the Reds were behind, 18-0. McKechnie mercifully pulled his 15-year-old from the game.

Joe didn't pitch again in the majors until 1952. He won a career-high 17 games in 1955 and pitched 3⅓ scoreless innings in that year's All-Star Game. He retired just before Opening Day 1967 and has been a Reds broadcaster since.

"I could have pitched for the Reds when I was even younger — at 14 — but I turned 'em down," Joe said. "My junior high basketball team was on a roll, and I didn't want to miss playing in any of their games."

Nuxhall was discovered by accident.

"A Reds scout came to Hamilton to watch my dad, Orville, pitch in a semipro game," Joe said. "Several games were going on at adjacent fields. The scout happened to spot me. He liked what he saw, and he forgot about signing my dad."

The name of the street that runs past that field was changed from Ford Boulevard to Joe Nuxhall Boulevard.

Nuxhall has made Hamilton proud. He is a great partner for the highly talented Marty Brennaman. Joe's warm and friendly down-home appeal has won thousands of hearts.

The 15-year-old kid who fell on his face that June afternoon has become a big man in Reds history.

Originally printed on June 17, 1994

Detroiter turned a slight into a crusade

It was an exciting moment for young Wendell Smith from Detroit's Southeastern High School. He had pitched his American Legion team to a 1-0 victory; his catcher, Mike Tresh, and other teammates were hugging him and lifting him onto their shoulders.

The famous Tigers scout, Wish Egan, came out of the stands.

"Great game, kid," he told Smith. "You beat a good pitcher. I'm trying to sign him and your catcher, Tresh, too. I wish I could sign you, but I can't."

Wendell knew the reason. He was black. This was 1930, 17 years before Jackie Robinson.

"That broke me up," Smith recalled. "Right then I made a vow that I would dedicate myself to doing something on behalf of the Negro ballplayers. That was one of the reasons I became a sports writer."

On July 31, Smith was inducted posthumously into the writers' wing of the Hall of Fame as the 1994 recipient of the J.G. Taylor Spink Award.

Smith wrote sports for the Pittsburgh Courier, the Chicago American and Sun Times and later worked for WGN-TV. The first black member of the Baseball Writers Association of America, Smith died in 1972 at age 58.

No sports writer had a greater influence on the integration of baseball. Wendell was the choice of

Branch Rickey to room with Jackie Robinson and smooth Jackie's path to big-league stardom.

Smith was a great athlete at Southeastern High, where he was an all-city basketball player and baseball player.

"I grew up in Detroit, in an all-white neighborhood," Smith said. "I was the only Negro in Southeastern High."

Wendell's father was born in Dresden, Ontario. He started as a dishwasher on the boats running from Detroit to Buffalo. He later became a chef for Henry Ford.

"When I was a kid — around 10 or 11 — my father started taking me to the Ford mansion," Smith recalled. "I knew all the youngsters. Edsel, Benson and Henry used to play a lot of baseball with me."

After graduating from West Virginia State College, Smith began writing sports in 1937 for the Pittsburgh Courier. Within a year, Smith had become sports editor and began a campaign to bring blacks into the big leagues.

In 1945, Smith implored the Red Sox to stage tryouts for three black players: Jackie Robinson, Marvin Williams and Sam Jethroe. He never heard from Boston officials, but a first step had been taken.

Originally printed on May 13, 1994

Song remained
the same for Caray

Harry Caray was a major league broadcaster
for 53 seasons. To put it in perspective,
Connie Mack and Nick Altrock were the
only baseball figures who served longer than Caray.

Mack put in 61 years as a player and manager.
Altrock was a player and coach for 55. Next on the
list comes Jimmy Dykes, with 45 years of service as
player, coach and manager.

Caray, who was baseball broadcasting's premier
showman, broke in with the St. Louis Cards in 1945.
He left St. Louis after the '69 season for one year in
Oakland and then went to Chicago, where he broadcast the White Sox and Cubs.

I met Caray in 1948, when I was announcing for
the Brooklyn Dodgers. He was a great friend and
loyal supporter. When Harry suffered a serious
stroke that kept him off the air a good part of the
1987 season, he asked me — among others — to substitute for him on WGN-TV. With Steve Stone, I
telecast a Cubs game from Veterans Stadium in
Philadelphia. Through eight innings, Cubs left-hander Jamie Moyer was pitching a no-hitter. But Juan
Samuel led off the ninth with a single and spoiled
the bid.

"I knew Moyer wouldn't get that no-hitter," I told
Stone. "Harry would never allow anything like that
without being here to call it himself."

In '48, Harry and Gabby Street were the Cards' announcers and Harry's 9-year-old son Skip was hanging around the radio booth. Skip is now the veteran announcer in Atlanta and Skip's son Chip is announcing Cubs games on WGN.

It's a great story of three generations of Carays.

I was on an ESPN show with Harry and Bob Murphy, the Mets' announcer. I told Harry I was envious that he benefited from the greatest gimmick in baseball-announcing history: singing the national anthem in the seventh inning of every Cubs game.

Harry told me he couldn't take credit for that one. Instead, it came as a stroke of genius by the late Bill Veeck, then the White Sox owner.

Here's the way Caray told it:

"My first five years with the White Sox I'd sing 'Take Me Out to the Ball Game' in the booth during the seventh inning. Nobody heard it but my partner, Jimmy Piersall. Then Bill Veeck bought the ballclub. The first night he owned the team he looked over to my booth and saw me singing the song. He also saw that fans in front of the booth joined in.

"Next night, Veeck hid the PA mike in my booth. It picked up my singing and the whole crowd joined in. After the game I asked Veeck, 'What was that all about?'

" 'Harry,' Veeck said, 'when I heard you sing, I knew you were the guy I was looking for. Anybody who heard you had to know he could sing better than you and he would be sure to join in.' "

So let's all stand for a musical tribute to Harry

Caray. Fifty-three years of big-league announcing is something to sing about.

Originally printed on April 15, 1994

Seeing Mays' debut was my privilege

One of the greatest thrills for a broadcaster is to watch an outstanding rookie break into the major leagues. If that rookie goes on to reach the Hall of Fame, the thrill becomes a treasured memory.

In my broadcasting career, I've seen many Hall of Famers make their debuts: Eddie Mathews, Luis Aparicio, Rod Carew, Brooks Robinson, Reggie Jackson, Harmon Killebrew, to name a few.

But my super thrill came when I watched a 20-year-old kid from Alabama, Willie Mays, bat for the first time. Willie's debut was even more exciting for me because he was playing for the team for which I was broadcasting, the New York Giants.

Willie's first year in the big leagues was 1951, but I had heard about him the year before when he had started his career at Trenton, N.J. Willie hit .353 in 81 games there, and in the spring of 1951 the Giants were touting him as their best prospect.

Owner Horace Stoneham and manager Leo Durocher left training camp in St. Petersburg and drove to Sanford, Fla., to see Willie in a morning intrasquad game. Mays hit a double and a home run, threw out two runners from centerfield and stole a base. After seven innings, Stoneham and Durocher left. They had seen enough to know this kid was something special.

"One year in the minors," Leo told us when he got back to St. Pete. "After that, he'll be a Giant. Can't miss."

The Giants started slowly and needed help. Leo was so high on Mays that he convinced Stoneham to bring him up to the Giants in late May. The youngster was hitting .477 at Minneapolis, and the fans loved his exciting acrobatics in the outfield.

Minneapolis was playing at Sioux City, Iowa. The Giants couldn't find Mays at his hotel, but traced him to a movie theater. In the middle of the film, Mays was surprised to see a message on the screen: "Willie Mays, call your hotel."

The Giants were playing the Phillies at Shibe Park when Willie reported for his first game. I remember him in batting practice; we all stopped to look at his swings. Not only the media, but players of both teams gathered to watch. He pounded several long drives over the fence, and it didn't take a genius to know that this 20-year-old was super.

Durocher put him in the lineup right away. Mays was hitless in five at-bats during that first game. When we left Philadelphia for New York, he was 0-for-12. I remember that train ride. Monte Irvin sat with Mays and tried to convince him the major leagues weren't that tough.

The next game was against the Boston Braves at the Polo Grounds. Before that May 28 game, a scared and befuddled Mays entered Durocher's office.

"Mr. Leo," he said, "I can't play up here. I want to go back to Minneapolis."

"Never happen, Willie," Durocher said. "As long as I'm manager here, you're my centerfielder. I know you can do the job; now go out there tonight and do it."

In the first inning, Mays hit a home run over the leftfield stands off Warren Spahn. Mays struggled some afterward, but was on his way to being named rookie of the year.

When I think about rookies breaking in, I remember Mays and how the faith of Durocher started him on the way to the Hall of Fame.

Originally printed on April 4, 1994

Ernie Harwell

Double triple crown
wasn't singled out in '33

Baseball has not had a Triple Crown winner since Boston's Carl Yastrzemski in 1967.

While checking on that, I discovered something that had escaped me. In 1933, there were two Triple Crown winners, and both came from the same city — Philadelphia. In the American League, Jimmie Foxx won the honor when he batted .356, hit 48 home runs and knocked in 163 runs. Chuck Klein took the Triple Crown in the National League; he hit .368 with 28 home runs and 120 RBIs.

If that double feat had happened in one city in our modern baseball era, there would be all kinds of excitement. The TV networks would break into their programming; ESPN would be churning out documentaries; and the headlines all over the nation would be screaming about Foxx and Klein.

To find out the impact of the double feat at the time, I checked the 1934 Reach Baseball Guide.

In the first eight pages of articles, the editor didn't mention Foxx or Klein. In the AL review of the 1933 season, Foxx's accomplishment was ignored. The NL review noted that Klein "led the league in batting and also took other hitting honors."

When the averages were analyzed, there were mentions of the two sluggers. One article pointed out that Foxx hit three home runs in one game and twice had five hits in a game. However, there was never any use of the term Triple Crown.

In review, I'd have to say that Klein and Foxx winning the Triple Crown in the same city was no big deal for their contemporaries.

For Foxx, winning the Triple Crown also led to his selection as the AL's most valuable player for the second straight season. Klein didn't fare as well; in the NL, the MVP went to New York Giants pitching great Carl Hubbell, who led the league with 23 wins, 10 shutouts and a 1.66 ERA in 308⅔ innings.

Klein was traded to the Cubs after the 1933 season and never again matched his exploits with the Phils. Foxx was unloaded to the Red Sox after the 1935 season, continued his slugging there, and finished with the Cubs and Phillies.

Jimmie's Triple Crown season of 1933 was no help to him financially. Connie Mack asked him that winter to take a pay cut from $16,333 to $12,000. Only after long and tough negotiations was Foxx finally able to maintain his salary.

Like the Reach Baseball Guide, Connie Mack felt that the Triple Crown — at least in the pocketbook — was no big deal.

If two sluggers from the same city won the Triple Crown in our times, it would be more than a big deal. It would be a sensation.

Originally printed on Sept. 24, 1993

Myths of the '27 Yanks greater than the team

When the Tigers began to show terrific power early in 1993, everybody began comparing them with the great 1927 New York Yankees. That team is considered by most baseball experts to be the greatest in history.

However, as in all history, baseball history often creates myths about teams and stars. In time, the margin between myth and truth seems to dim. Finally, we have difficulty separating the truth from the legend.

There are many myths about the great Yankees:

● 1. The 1927 Yankees were the first to be called "Murderers' Row."

Wrong! The Term "Murderers' Row" was given to the Yankees in 1919 by Robert Ripley. Even before he started his "Believe It Or Not" cartoon, Ripley drew a sports cartoon of Frank Baker, Roger Peckinpaugh, Wally Pipp and Del Pratt and dubbed them "Murderers' Row."

● 2. Yankees owner Jacob Ruppert put his players in pinstripe uniforms to fashion a slimmer look for an overweight Babe Ruth.

Wrong! The New Yorkers first wore pinstripes April 22, 1915, five years before Ruth joined them.

● 3. Ruth called his famous 1932 World Series home run off pitcher Charlie Root.

Wrong! Doubtful testimony dims the truth. In

overkill, it is baseball's answer to unending investigation of the John F. Kennedy assassination.

● 4. The 1927 Yankees had baseball's best-ever record.

Wrong! The Yankees' 110-44 record doesn't even hold the American League record. That belongs to the Cleveland Indians of 1954, who won 111 and lost 43. The major league record was set by the 1906 Chicago Cubs. They won 116 and lost 36.

● 5. All of the 1927 Yanks were superstars.

Wrong! Ruth, Lou Gehrig, Earle Combs, Tony Lazzeri, Herb Pennock and Waite Hoyt are Hall of Famers from that team — managed by Miller Huggins, another Hall of Famer — but even the great teams have unknowns. Ray Morehart, a reserve infielder, batted .256, hit one home run and knocked in 20 runs. The Yanks had three catchers, none of them outstanding: Pat Collins, John Grabowski and Benny Bengough. Some other filler-inners were Mike Gazella, Cedric Durst and Myles Thomas.

● 6. When Ruth hit 60 home runs in 1927, several of his homers bounced into the stands.

Wrong! It is true that a bounce-in drive was a home run in 1927, but careful research has revealed that all of Ruth's 60 homers reached the seats or beyond on the fly.

● 7. Ruth hit three home runs for the Boston Braves at Pittsburgh in the final three times at bat in his career.

Wrong! Those homers were the Babe's last hurrah. But he played several games after that and retired five days after his Pittsburgh performance.

● 8. The 1927 Yankees drew tremendous crowds.

Wrong! Yankees teams in 1920 (1,289,422) and 1921 (1,230,696) outdrew the '27 team, which attracted 1,164,015. The best-drawing team in Yankees history was the 1988 club, which attracted 2,633,701.

● 9. Gehrig's streak of 2,130 straight regular-season games — out of the 2,164 in his career — began when he replaced Wally Pipp at first base after Pipp's famous headache.

Wrong! Gehrig had started his streak the day before, June 1, 1925, with a pinch-hit. Also, he had appeared in 23 games for New York in 1923-24.

Editor's note: Since this column was printed on July 23, 1993, the 1999 Yankees have become the best-drawing team in club history, attracting 3,292,736.

Ernie Harwell

Tigers Tales

MARY SCHROEDER/Detroit Free Press

Aurelio (Senor Smoke) Lopez was the Tigers' first set-up man, who, by a strange twist of fate, met his death almost eight years to the day and in similar fashion to . . .

Detroit Free Press file photo

. . . Aurelio Rodriguez, the Tigers' third baseman for nine seasons who also was killed in a car accident. I have fond memories of the two personable and outgoing players.

Rodriguez and Lopez are forever linked

The death of Aurelio Rodriguez brought an ironic twist. It meant that two Tigers stars from Mexico — Rodriguez and Aurelio Lopez — had died in tragic accidents.

Both were named Aurelio.

Both died pinned under autos.

And both died in late September.

Rodriguez's accident occurred Sept. 23, 2000. Lopez was killed Sept. 22, 1992, when he was thrown from a chauffeur-driven car that had crashed in Mexico.

Lopez, nicknamed Senor Smoke, won his place in Tigers history as the team's first set-up man. His mid-inning relief heroics paved the way for Detroit's super closer and Cy Young Award winner, Willie Hernandez.

I have fond memories of Lopez and Rodriguez. Both were personable and outgoing. But most of my memories are away from the diamond.

Rodriguez played third base for nine seasons in Detroit, longer than any other third baseman in team history. After he had become an established star, I received a letter from a longtime fan. It read:

"Dear Ernie, Last week I took my 8-year-old grandson to Tiger Stadium. When he saw Aurelio Rodriguez, he turned to me and said, 'Grandpa, that Rodriguez doesn't look so old to me.'

"What do you mean?" I asked.

"Well," he said, "Ernie Harwell is always saying on the radio that he is a really old Rodriguez."

My recollection of Aurelio Lopez also is a personal vignette. I had often wondered about the briefcases players used to take on trips. It's not true anymore, but when Lopez was pitching, all the players toted briefcases on the planes and buses.

"What do those contain?" I asked myself. "Are they jammed with business documents, ledgers and letters?" One day in Kansas City I found my answer.

We had flown from Chicago to Kansas City after a day game. I was sitting on the team bus at the Kansas City airport, watching the players get on the bus. Here comes Lopez, carrying the ubiquitous briefcase. Just before he reaches the door of the bus, he drops his briefcase. It springs open, and the entire contents fall out onto the sidewalk. The entire contents? Only one item — a small bottle of Tabasco sauce. At that moment, I knew why the players needed those briefcases.

Originally printed on Sept. 30, 2000

MARY SCHROEDER/Detroit Free Press

Sparky Anderson always understood the mind of the baseball fan and the player.

Ernie Harwell

Sparky always had a special touch

Everybody has a Sparky Anderson story. I have two, and each reflects his human touch — one with his players and one with his public.

When Sparky's Reds played the Orioles in the 1970 World Series, he had a second-string catcher named Pat Corrales. In his third year of backing up Johnny Bench, Corrales was finishing the sixth year of his nine-year undistinguished career.

The Orioles were leading the series, three games to one. The final game at Baltimore's Memorial Stadium found the Birds ahead, 9-3, in the ninth. It was all over — just a matter of three more outs. Mike Cuellar retired the first two Reds easily. One to go and the Orioles were champions.

Corrales was watching from the dugout. It was his first World Series and his last. Anderson looked down the bench toward Corrales.

"Pat," he told him, "get up there and hit for Hal McRae. You deserve to be in a World Series, and this might be your only chance."

Pat grounded out to third baseman Brooks Robinson and the series was over. But he had batted in a World Series — thanks to a thoughtful manager.

My other Anderson story happened in 1984, the year the Tigers started 35-5. Sparky's team had won

104

17 consecutive road games. His picture graced the covers of magazines, and his name was in headlines across the country. He and I were having breakfast at our Anaheim hotel when a fan approached our table.

"Hi, Sparky," he said. "I'm a great fan of yours. I live in San Diego now, but I was living in Cincinnati when you managed that Big Red Machine. You have always been my hero. Without a doubt you are the greatest manager ever."

Sparky beamed. Silently, he listened and just nodded his head. Then, the man spoke again.

"And by the way, Sparky, what are you doing these days?"

Sparky gave him a polite smile and returned to his eggs and bacon.

But that fan's question gave Anderson a conversation topic for the rest of the trip. Sparky always understood the mind of the baseball fan and the player.

Originally printed on July 20, 2000

Detroit Free Press file photo

Willie Horton deserves all the accolades for his play. But Horton also could have won the award for the Tigers' biggest hypochondriac.

Horton's theatrics were as good as his play

Today is Willie Horton's day. I'm pleased he is being honored at Comerica Park with a much-deserved statue and the retirement of his Tigers No. 23. Willie is Detroit's own — a wonderful man and true friend.

If life is a landscape, Willie is a garden of emotions. The centerpiece of his garden is a blooming hypochondria. You won't find that flower listed in seed catalogs and it might not be in everybody's garden. But during his baseball career, it was a thriving example of Willie's way.

Horton never met an ailment he didn't anguish about. Always treating each ache or pain with an overdose of exaggeration, he was the Tigers' Moaner Lisa. To Willie, a simple headache loomed as a brain tumor. The sniffles indicated at least pneumonia, and a boil on his leg meant immediate amputation.

One afternoon at Tiger Stadium, Willie made a diving catch in leftfield, suffering an injured leg. Rolling over on his back, he looked to the heavens and shouted for help.

Judging by his theatrics, you quickly discerned that leftfield had qualified as Willie's deathbed. Here is the unforgettable scene we saw that afternoon.

Trainer Bill Behm struggles up the dugout steps to begin his slow gallop toward Horton.

Here comes manager Mayo Smith to check on his suffering slugger. Mayo's sprint onto the field can't equal his usual speed to the buffet or bar — the only places he has been training for the past 20 years. On the way toward Willie, Smith suddenly goes down. A leg cramp has sent him sprawling off the turf.

Trainer Behm faces a dilemma. Horton is almost near death — at least in Willie's mind. On the other hand, Behm's manager and boss is suffering with his charley horse and demanding attention.

The answer's obvious: attend the boss.

So, Wondrous Willie is treated second. He recovers and lives to play leftfield for the Tigers.

Because he has always been one of my favorites, I'm certainly happy that Willie survived.

Originally printed on July 15, 2000

Ernie Harwell

Classy pro Kaline tops my Tigers

As it approaches the unknown seas of the millennium, the good ship U.S. Journalism is listing. Never have so many lists unbalanced so many readers. I join the listing with my list of 10 top Tigers. These are stars I have seen play during my almost 40 years at the microphone with the club.

1. Al Kaline: The consummate pro for 22 seasons. A brilliant fielder and clutch hitter. Too bad this great team player appeared in only one World Series.

2. Alan Trammell and Lou Whitaker: They make the list as one. Baseball's most enduring keystone combination. For almost 20 years together, they were the heart and soul of their teams.

3. Bill Freehan: He caught more games than any other Tiger. A steady force behind the plate and a top-notch leader. Always there with big clutch hits.

4. Lance Parrish: Freehan's equal in his own generation. He always put his team first.

5. Mark Fidrych: The most charismatic of all the Tigers. The Bird was always good for another 20,000 at the game — home or away. It was a shame injuries shortened his colorful career.

6. Cecil Fielder: The big guy was underrated. He was the most powerful Tiger of our era. Until Mark McGwire, I never had seen anybody hit a ball harder.

7. Denny McLain: His 31-victory season in 1968 ranks No. 1 for a single-season performance. Despite his shortcomings and off-the-field problems, McLain was a proven winner.

8. Mickey Lolich: Probably the most underrated Tigers pitcher. A true workhorse, he was effective as a starter and reliever. He never missed a turn and could always give you 200 to 300 innings a season.

9. Jack Morris: My top gamer. He proved his worth as a winning pitcher under playoff and World Series pressure. The competitive juices flowed freely in the tightly wound Mr. Morris.

10. Willie Hernandez: The classic reliever. In 1984 he won the Cy Young and MVP awards after saving 32 games in 33 opportunities for the World Series champions. No Detroit bullpen star was any better for one season than Hernandez.

Those are my 10. Is your list any better?

Originally printed on Sept. 14, 1999

How scouts rated Kaline and Gibby

As I was rummaging through old papers I found an article I had written about Al Kaline for the Sporting News of Jan. 10, 1962. Al was 27 years old and about to enter his 10th season as a Tiger. My story focused on the Tigers' scouting report of Al when he was a 15-year-old high schooler in Baltimore. Scout Ed Katalinas provided me with that original assessment of the future Hall of Famer.

The 1950 report said this about Kaline:

1. Showed outstanding arm.
2. Has good speed.
3. Excellent body control.
4. Natural outfielder (CF).
5. Best kid player I ever scouted.
6. Have four years to watch develop.

One of Kaline's neighbors gave Katalinas the first tip on Kaline. Ed had signed a young Baltimore shortstop named Charlie Johnson.

"Mr. Katalinas, there's a young fellow who lives near here you should see," Johnson told Ed. "His name is Kaline. He's only about 15, but he'll be a great player someday."

Ed scouted Kaline for four years and signed him to a Tigers contract in 1953, the day after he graduated from Southern High School.

Let's fast-forward to another scouting report.

This time it's about Kaline's TV potential. I wrote this about my TV partner: "Last October he appeared on a Detroit TV show before each World Series game, interviewing players from the area and commenting on the games. He was warm and made a fine impression."

Having checked on Kaline, I decided to pursue a scouting report on my other TV partner, Kirk Gibson. Through Erikka Cullum of the Tigers' public relations office, I got in touch with Sharon Arend, who is company historian for Little Caesars and heads up the archives for all the Ilitch-owned entities. She dug up three scouting reports on Gibson.

All three reports were from the Major League Scouting Bureau. Their scouts had checked Gibson in March, April and May 1978, his junior year at Michigan State. Their grading key, based on major league standards, ranged from three (well below average) to eight (outstanding). The first scout was Lenny Merullo. His ratings went this way: "Arm — three; field — four (below average); running speed — eight; hit — three, and power — seven (very good)."

A month later, scout Jim Martz turned in his report. He gave Gibby a three in arm, field and hit. He rated eight in running speed and power. Very close to Merullo's report.

The third analysis came from Bob Sullivan and Jim Command. Except for running speed, they gave Gibson a better grade. He got fours in arm, field and running speed. For hitting, he got a six and for power he was awarded an eight.

The reports from Martz and Sullivan-Command rated Kirk as a definite major league prospect. Merullo listed him as a fringe major leaguer. The Tigers signed Gibby as their No. 1 draft pick in June 1978.

Gibson and Kaline reached baseball stardom. Both are stars in the TV booth. I'm lucky to have such talented partners.

And now you know how the scouts rated them before they began their outstanding careers.

Originally printed on May 29, 1998

Tettleton made best of second chance

The start of the 1988 season was two days away. Triple-A Rochester manager Johnny Oates desperately needed a catcher, and Mickey Tettleton — just released by Oakland — needed a job.

Tettleton — who retired in 1997 — got that job and a new future with Oates.

"My release was rough to take," Tettleton recalled, "but getting with Oates at Rochester was the best thing that ever happened to me."

Tettleton caught and played outfield at Rochester. The Orioles — off to an 0-21 start — called him up after 19 games.

"My career turned around," said Tettleton, now 41. "Because of the bad start, our manager, Frank Robinson, gave me a chance to play."

In 1989, Tettleton's home run prowess — and Froot Loops — brought him cult status. A TV announcer asked Sylvia, Mickey's wife, why he was hitting so many home runs.

"He's eating Froot Loops now," she said.

The next afternoon, a huge Froot Loops banner appeared in the rightfield stands and the loopy Froot Loops cult took off.

After another productive season at Baltimore, Tettleton came to Detroit in a trade for pitcher Jeff Robinson. He had four solid seasons with the Tigers, winning admiration from teammates for dedicated play.

"Mickey is the ideal team man," Alan Trammell said. "He played for us when he was hurt, but he was always ready."

Teammate Cecil Fielder agreed.

"He was one of my closest friends," Fielder said. "He was valuable because he was a productive hitter who could play many positions."

Tettleton missed his Tigers pals but was pleased to be in Texas for the last three seasons of his career.

When Oates became manager at Texas, he asked general manager Doug Melvin to get Tettleton, who had not re-signed with the Tigers. Because of salary restraints, chances were slim. But after a stint at a free-agent camp in Homestead, Fla., and a nerve-wrenching wait, Tettleton signed with the Rangers on April 13, 1995.

Tettleton continued to put heavy stats next to his name. For the Rangers he had 59 home runs, 165 RBIs and 259 walks.

"Mickey knows the difference between pain and discomfort," Oates said. "You don't beg him to go on the field, you have to pull him off it."

Originally printed on May 3, 1996

Brookens' catching saved the day

I've known hundreds of Tigers players. I've tolerated some, enjoyed the company of most, and truly admired a few.

One of my favorites is Tom Brookens, the man I dubbed the Pennsylvania Poker.

Brookens had a great sense of humor, an honest outlook, and was one of the most personable Tigers.

He's retired now in Fayetteville, Pa.

"Saying retired," Brookens said, "sounds better than unemployed. I do a little construction work, take care of my three daughters, and hunt and fish. I did coach some baseball, but now I'm the groundskeeper for our local sandlot teams."

Brookens hasn't returned to Tiger Stadium since he retired with Cleveland in 1990, but he follows the team via radio and the box scores.

The highlight that demonstrated his team spirit came in a game against Texas at Tiger Stadium on July 20, 1985.

Regular catcher Lance Parrish was injured, so Bob Melvin started behind the plate. After Melvin left for pinch-hitter Alex Sanchez, infielder Marty Castillo was pressed into catching.

Johnny Grubb pinch-hit for Castillo in the 10th inning, scoring Chet Lemon with a sacrifice fly that tied the score at 4.

Brookens, on first base at the time, turned to

first-base coach Dick Tracewski and said, "Trixie, if we tie this game, we don't have another catcher."

"Oh, yes we do," Tracewski said, staring at Brookens.

When Brookens reached the dugout, manager Sparky Anderson asked, "Tom, can you catch?"

Brookens said: "I've never done it — not even in Little League — but I'll give it a try."

Brookens donned the equipment, but it was much too big. He wandered behind the plate, wondering what would happen.

"My concern was not to embarrass myself and the team," said Brookens, the regular third base-man. "I was lucky that Aurelio Lopez came in to pitch at the same time. He was easy to catch. He had great control and didn't throw any trick pitches."

When Brookens reached the plate, umpire Ken Kaiser asked, "What the hell are you doing here?"

"I'm catching," Brookens said.

"Ever caught before?" Kaiser asked.

"No," Brookens said.

"I don't feel too good about this," Kaiser said. "Please don't get me killed."

After Brookens caught the first pitch, he felt better. On the next pitch, the batter swung and missed. Brookens caught that one and felt even better.

"I knew nothing about calling pitches," he said. "Lopez just kept throwing fastballs. Now and then he would shake me off."

Brookens went to the mound and asked Lopez why he was shaking him off.

"It doesn't mean a thing," Lopez told him. "I'm

just trying to confuse the hitters."

"The guy you're confusing is me," Brookens told him.

When Brookens entered the dugout after one inning, he heard a teammate say, "Let's score a run so Brookie doesn't have to go back out there."

"I second it," Brookens said.

Lopez left after the 13th inning, and left-hander Bill Scherrer replaced him.

"By then I'd had a crash course in signal-calling," Brookens said. "Scherrer was harder to catch than Lopez, but we didn't have much trouble because he pitched away."

Only three Rangers reached base while Brookens was catching, and two stole second — one when Brookens dropped a pitch.

Finally in the 15th, Barbaro Garbey singled in Alan Trammell, giving the Tigers a 6-5 victory. When the Tigers trudged into the clubhouse, Parrish had a presentation for Brookens.

It was a catcher's mask filled with ice and two bottles of beer.

Originally printed on April 24, 1999

Opening Day memories at The Corner

I had been broadcasting big league baseball six years before I saw Detroit's famous corner, then called Briggs Stadium.

That experience came in 1954, when I debuted as the radio and TV voice of the Baltimore Orioles. The Tigers' opener that season was the first Orioles game in modern major league history.

As a youngster in Atlanta, I had read many articles about Briggs Stadium. During the Detroit-Cubs 1935 World Series, I subscribed to the Detroit Free Press and the Detroit News and had seen hundreds of photographs of that famous baseball landmark.

Yet my first look overwhelmed me. The stadium loomed in the sky like a huge battleship.

The Tigers' Steve Gromek beat Baltimore, 3-0, in that '54 opener — my first ever at the corner of Michigan and Trumbull. The Orioles won the next game and took the train to Baltimore for their historic home opener.

My first opener as a Tigers broadcaster came on the road in 1960. George Kell and I froze for 14 innings in 36-degree temperatures as the Tigers defeated the Cleveland Indians.

For the home opener, Detroit basked in a contrasting 80-degree, sunny afternoon. My most vivid memory of that day was our TV interview with White Sox second baseman Nelson Fox. When Kell and I finished our chat with Nellie, the director told us the tape was faulty.

"Do it again," he said.

We did. But again the taping went wrong. We had to ask Fox to undergo a third take, and he graciously agreed.

That was my first of 38 home openers as a Tigers announcer.

Some other home opener memories include:

Frank Lary, the famed "Yankee Killer," hurting his leg in a slide into third base against New York in 1962. The Tigers won, 5-3, but Lary was never the same after his injury.

Dwight Evans' home run off Jack Morris' first pitch in 1986. The drive reached the leftfield stands even before most of the crowd of 51,437 had settled into their seats. The Tigers came back and won, 6-5, on a big day for Kirk Gibson, who went 4-for-4 with two homers and five RBIs.

The centerfield smash off Larry Herndon's bat in 1987. It hit the facing of the upper-deck centerfield bleachers. It was the only Tigers run in their 2-1 loss to New York.

Now, another opener, our last at the old ballpark.

Originally printed on April 12, 1999

Happy 100th at The Corner

Michigan's most famous sports corner cele-
brated its 100th birthday April 28, 1996.

On the afternoon of April 28, 1896, the
Tigers beat the Columbus Senators, 17-2, in the first
game at Bennett Park, the forerunner to Tiger
Stadium. Baseball has been played at that site
longer than at any other park.

For almost 50 years, the Woodbridge Grove at the
corner of Michigan and Trumbull had been a popular place for families to picnic. Tigers owner George
Arthur Vanderbeck decided he would leave the
cramped little baseball field in east Detroit and
build a new park at this location.

Many trees had been cut down, and the city had
established a hay market for farmers. During the
winter of 1895-96, Vanderbeck, began to build his
new park. He spent $10,000 to cover the market's
cobblestones with dirt and sod. He built a grandstand and bleachers. The seating capacity was
5,000.

At first, the park was called Haymarket or
Woodbridge Grove, but after a few years it became
known as Bennett Park in honor of Charlie Bennett,
star catcher of Detroit's National League champions
of 1887. Charlie had lost his legs in an 1894 train accident.

On Opening Day, Bennett was the catcher as
Wayne County treasurer Alex McLeod threw out
the ceremonial first pitch. A terrific cannon boom

lent a festive air to the park dedication.

The first pitch, by Jack Fifield, was thrown to a Columbus batter named Campbell.

In the bottom of the first inning, George Stallings of the Tigers hit a long fly to centerfield. The Columbus centerfielder, Butler, gave chase. But Butler collided with a spectator on the outfield grass, and Stallings circled the bases with the first home run at Michigan and Trumbull.

In those days, the Tigers were not in the majors. They had just left the National League to become a member of Ban Johnson's newly formed Western League. In 1901, Johnson restructured his organization to form the American League.

The Tigers played all home games at Bennett except on Sundays. Because of the blue laws, they were forced to play Sunday games at Burns Park on Dix Avenue between Livernois and Waterman.

Later, Bennett Park became Navin Field, then Briggs Stadium and Tiger Stadium. There was baseball at Michigan and Trumbull until Sept. 28, 1999.

But on April 28, 1996, we toasted the most famous corner in Michigan sports and sang "Happy 100th Birthday" to Michigan and Trumbull.

Originally printed on April 26, 1996

By the numbers, '84 Tigers edge '68 team

WARNING: This column contains statistics. They may be harmful to the casual reader. You might know that I don't care for statistics. I think we have too many meaningless ones in baseball. However, today I'm making an exception in order to answer a question a fan asked on WDFN. The question: If the 1968 Tigers played the '84 Tigers, which team would win?

The only way to find an answer was to dig into the records and cite statistics. My conclusion: It would be a close matchup, but the 1984 team would win.

When you look over the figures, there is an amazing similarity between the teams.

The '68 team won 103 and lost 59. The '84 champs were 104-58. In '68, Baltimore, in second place, finished 12 games back. In '84, the runner-up Toronto Blue Jays were 15 back. Each Tigers team led the league in runs. It was 671 in '68 and 829 in '84. Each led in homers. The '68 team hit 185; the '84 group had 187. Neither team boasted a player with 100 RBIs. Jim Northrup, with 90, topped the '68 team; in '84, Kirk Gibson was the best with 91. Each team had a Cy Young Award winner and MVP. Denny McLain won both honors, and in '84 Willie Hernandez did it in relief.

A comparison, by position:

FIRST BASE: I'll take Norm Cash over Dave

Bergman. Bergman outhit Norm, .273 to .263, but Cash had 25 home runs and batted in 63 runs. Bergman had seven homers and 44 RBIs.

SECOND BASE: Lou Whitaker over Dick McAuliffe. Each knocked in 56 runs. Whitaker batted .289 to Mac's .249. McAuliffe outhomered Lou, 16 to 13, but Whitaker was a better fielder.

SHORTSTOP: Alan Trammell over Ray Oyler. Oyler batted only .135 with one home run and 12 RBIs. Trammell hit .314 with 14 homers and 69 RBIs. Trammell is the only regular who hit .300 for either Tigers team.

THIRD BASE: The statistics favor '84's Howard Johnson over Don Wert. However, I'll pick Wert because he was a much steadier fielder. Wert hit .200 with 12 home runs and 37 RBIs. Johnson batted .248, hit 12 home runs and knocked in 50.

LEFTFIELD: Willie Horton over Larry Herndon. Horton led the team in homers with 36. He batted .285, and his RBI total was 85. Herndon hit .280 with seven home runs and 43 RBIs.

CENTERFIELD: Chet Lemon was much stronger than Mickey Stanley in each batting department. He outhit Mickey, .287 to .259. He hit 20 homers to Stanley's 11. And his RBI total was 76 to Mickey's 60. Both were fine defensive players, but Stanley was much steadier. Lemon was a poor baserunner; Stanley had great baseball instincts. Even.

RIGHTFIELD: Kirk Gibson over Northrup. Gibson batted .282, had 27 home runs and 91 RBIs. Northrup hit .264 with 21 home runs and 90 RBIs. Northrup was the better defensive player.

CATCHER: Here's where I go against the stats: Bill Freehan over Lance Parrish. Lance had better power. He hit 33 homers to Freehan's 25. He knocked in 98 runs to Bill's 84. Freehan had the better average, .263 to .237. I take Freehan because he was such a superior defensive catcher.

PITCHING: A slight edge to the '68 team. McLain overshadows everybody with 31-6 and a 1.96 ERA. He pitched 336 innings. The '68 staff racked up 19 shutouts compared to eight for the '84 staff. Its ERA was 2.71; the ERA of the '84 team was 3.49.

The '84 pitching star was Hernandez. He was in 80 games, had a 1.92 ERA, won nine and lost three, and had 32 saves. Jack Morris was the super starter. He won 19 and lost 11 with a 3.60 ERA. Other '84 stalwarts were Dan Petry (18-8), Milt Wilcox (17-8) and Aurelio Lopez (10-1).

Besides McLain, the '68 regular starters were Mickey Lolich (17-9), Earl Wilson (13-12) and Joe Sparma (10-10). John Hiller (9-6) and Pat Dobson (5-8) did most of the relieving.

RESERVES: The '68 team had Al Kaline, who played in 102 games and hit .287. It also had the premier pinch-hitter, Gates Brown, who batted .370. However, the '84 Tigers had more bench strength. They boasted Tom Brookens, Ruppert Jones, Johnny Grubb, Marty Castillo and Rusty Kuntz.

MANAGER: Sparky Anderson over '68 skipper Mayo Smith. Anderson was much more into the game, more alert, and a much better strategist.

Originally printed on August 26, 1994

Off-season antics upset ump

Baseball's off-season is different than it was before big salaries. The modern player doesn't have to work and can spend his free time in a health club or in his personal gym. The old-time player either worked at selling cars or insurance, or maybe just had fun drinking and playing practical jokes.

One of my favorite stories about those off-season antics involves Herman (Germany) Schaefer, who played second base on the Tigers' pennant winners of 1907-09. Schaefer lived in Chicago and spent his winters hanging around a tavern called the Log Cabin Inn. One of his drinking pals was American League umpire Jack Sheridan.

One cold winter night, Germany found the ump sleeping in a chair leaned against the kitchen drain pipe. Schaefer climbed onto the roof and found the other end of the pipe. He shouted down into the sleeping umpire's ear, "Jack Sheridan, your time has came!"

Sheridan jumped from his chair and headed to the bar. He quickly downed a couple of whiskeys and asked himself if he had heard a warning voice or if those onions and pig knuckles had attacked his psyche.

Awhile later he was back in his chair, dozing again. Again Schaefer climbed up to the roof and shouted down the pipe, "Jack Sheridan, your time has came!"

Sheridan bolted from his chair and ran past the bar into the night. He didn't return to the Log Cabin the rest of that off-season.

The story doesn't end until the following summer. It's a hot August afternoon at Bennett Park in Detroit. Only 300 fans are watching the Tigers struggle through a dreary game. They are losing, but no one seems to care. Sheridan is umpiring behind the plate. Schaefer comes to bat. The pitcher throws a curve, which misses the plate.

"Strike one!" Sheridan says. Germany gives him a dirty look, but says nothing.

Here comes another pitch. It's two feet outside. "Strike two!" Sheridan shouts.

Schaefer is steaming. But he doesn't turn to protest. Instead, for the third time in his life, Sheridan hears that terrible warning: "Jack Sheridan, your time has came!"

The umpire is stunned by that echo from the winter past. "So it was you, you Dutch so-and-so!" he shouts as he swings his fist at Schaefer and misses. He kicks at him and misses.

"You're out of the game!" Sheridan yells. He chases Schaefer all the way to the clubhouse, then ejects him for his antics of the winter before, plus his summertime reminder.

Originally printed on Oct. 7, 2000

Intangibles paid off for Gibson

Kirk Gibson brought to the Tigers an unusual quality — "intangibles," Branch Rickey used to say.

Rickey, baseball's smartest executive, had a deep appreciation for the combination of temperament, aggressiveness and spirit Gibson personifies.

One of Rickey's favorites was Eddie Stanky, about whom he said, "He can't hit, throw or run, but I'd rather have him on my team than almost any other player."

Gibson possesses more talent than Stanky, but he is still the same type. His heroics in the 1988 World Series epitomized that.

Hobbled by a bad knee, Gibson left the trainer's table and hit a two-run pinch-hit homer off Oakland's Dennis Eckersley. That two-out blow in the ninth inning gave the Dodgers a Game 1 victory.

Baseball was sort of an afterthought for Gibson. His game was football, and he starred at Michigan State.

Unlike most big-leaguers, he played little baseball in his boyhood. He didn't play in college until his junior year. Danny Litwhiler, Michigan State's baseball coach, persuaded Kirk to give it a try.

There was some talk — never confirmed — that Gibby simply wanted to escape spring football practice. Anyway, he made the team, and despite an injured wrist, he was in the starting lineup when the season began.

But he could not buy a hit and was a picture of frustration. Gibby would strike out and return to the dugout muttering.

"Why did I ever get myself into this?" he asked.

After 12 straight at-bats without a hit, he went to Litwhiler.

"Coach," he said, "I don't need this aggravation. I can't hit. I don't think I'll ever hit."

"Wait, now, Kirk," Danny told him. "Just stick with it. You'll get started. You're too good to be doing this bad."

The next at-bat, Gibson hit a home run. He was on his way — home run after home run. Eventually, with little playing experience, he developed into a top collegiate prospect.

Gibson eschewed the NFL to sign with the Tigers as their first pick in the June 1978 draft. He played fewer than 150 games in the minors and came to the big leagues to stay in September 1979. He retired after the 1995 season.

Originally printed on May 6, 1994

My all-time Tigers, picked using my rules

During my 34 years of Tigers broadcasting, I've often been asked to name an all-time Tigers team. So I'm going to do it.

My selections will be restricted to those players I've seen in action from 1960 through the 1993 season. You'll likely disagree with my picks, and that's what makes it fun.

My first baseman is Norman Cash. He was a batting champion with home run power. I'll pick another first baseman, Cecil Fielder, who hits the ball harder and farther than anybody I've ever seen.

Second base belongs to Lou Whitaker. Steadiness and longevity put him on my team. Lou is underrated as a hitter. In the clutch or with two strikes on him, he is one of the best.

I have no doubts about shortstop. It has to be Alan Trammell. Tram does everything well. He will lead the team in batting this year for the seventh time in the past 14 years. His shortstop play is as consistent as I've ever seen.

At third, I debated but decided to take Aurelio Rodriguez over Don Wert. Both were good. But Rodriguez had a better arm — a true rifle — and was a better hitter than Don. I always felt that Aurelio, with his great arm, should have switched to pitching.

My outfield would consist of Al Kaline, Willie

Horton and Rocky Colavito. Kaline, the Hall of Famer, was the consummate professional. He was a consistent hitter who often could supply the home run. Nobody in my American League time ever played rightfield better than Al. Horton was less talented in the field but was a powerful clutch hitter. He contributed many clutch Tigers RBIs. And don't knock the Rock. Colavito was one of the Tigers' most colorful stars. His home run power was awesome, and he had an outstanding arm.

I'll take two catchers, Bill Freehan and Lance Parrish. Bill lasted longer and was probably better on defense. He also was a great leader. Parrish could throw well and gave the Tigers consistent longball power.

Because it's my team and I can do what I want, I am going to pick three starting pitchers and three relievers. My right-handers are Denny McLain and Jack Morris. Denny was sensational in 1968 with 31 victories, including one in the World Series. He followed the next year with 24. And he won 20 games in 1966.

Jack Morris lasted longer with the Tigers and through the years was a more dominant pitcher. He was the team's ultimate stopper.

My left-hander is Mickey Lolich, 1968 World Series hero with three victories over the St. Louis Cardinals. Mickey was a true workhorse. He pitched more than 300 innings in four straight seasons, and in 1971 and '72 won 25 and 22 games, respectively.

For my bullpen, I pick Mike Henneman, who set the all-time Tigers save record; John Hiller, the left-handed ace in the 1960s and '70s; and Guillermo Hernandez, who helped the Tigers to a Series title with his 32 saves in 1984.

For my pinch-hitter, my choice is Gates Brown. He handled the toughest job in baseball in great style and is certainly the best Tiger I ever saw in that role.

That's my team.

Originally printed on Oct. 1, 1993

Kuenn adds class to Michigan Hall

Baseball could not send a better representative than Harvey Kuenn to the Michigan Sports Hall of Fame.

In Detroit, we will remember Kuenn as a rookie-of-the-year shortstop for the 1953 Tigers and the 1959 American League batting champion.

In Milwaukee, Kuenn became manager of the Brewers in June 1982 and led his team to its only American League pennant.

Kuenn was a hard-nosed player and a no-nonsense manager. His teammates respected him, and the athletes who played for him had a true devotion to him.

That championship Brewers team was the pride of Kuenn's career. It slammed 216 home runs and had the nickname "Harvey's Wallbangers." Kuenn was named manager of the year by the Associated Press and United Press International.

Kuenn also had a personal triumph over physical hardships. The word "courage" truly fit him.

Harvey suffered a heart attack in 1976. He also had major stomach surgery, and his right leg was amputated below the knee.

Through it all, he kept his spirit and sense of humor. He never asked for pity or special favors.

Kuenn, born in West Allis, Wis., excelled in basketball and baseball at the University of Wisconsin.

He signed a bonus contract with the Tigers in 1952, spending his only minor league season at Davenport, Iowa.

In Kuenn's first full season, 1953, he was named rookie of the year by the Sporting News and the Baseball Writers' Association of America. He led the league in hits (209) and at-bats (679), and still holds AL rookie records for at-bats and singles (167).

Tigers Hall of Famer Al Kaline has fond memories of his early years with Kuenn.

"When I joined the Tigers," Al recalled, "Harvey looked after me. We were both young, and he made me feel that I was part of the team.

"It seemed that he could hit a line drive almost anytime he wanted. ... He never cared who was pitching; he knew he could hit. He was one of the best strike-two hitters I ever saw."

Kuenn spent eight years with the Tigers and made the All-Star team eight times (there were two games in 1959). He batted more than .300 his first four full seasons. His .353 average won the American League batting title in 1959.

At the close of spring training in 1960, Kuenn was traded by the Tigers to Cleveland for Rocky Colavito. It was a blockbuster deal — Kuenn, the batting champion, for Colavito, who with 42 home runs had shared the American League HR title the previous season with Harmon Killebrew of Washington.

From Cleveland, Kuenn went on to play for the San Francisco Giants and Chicago Cubs. He finished his career in 1966 with the Philadelphia Phillies.

I can still picture Kuenn, leaning into a fastball and slapping a hard line drive to right.

Harvey Kuenn — a worthy addition to the Michigan Sports Hall of Fame.

Originally printed on May 14, 1993

Rip created a long tide of excellence

He was a 13-year-old towhead, living in Corktown with his mom and grandparents. He was the smallest for his age in the neighborhood, but the bigger kids let him tag along when they swept out Briggs Stadium after games.

Then one day he met Hank Greenberg. The big Tigers first baseman said: "Whitey, meet me tomorrow morning at 10. I'm taking extra batting practice, and I want you to shag flies." That was Charles Frederick Collins' real introduction to the world of baseball. Almost 60 years later, he is still part of that world as custodian of the visitors clubhouse at Tiger Stadium.

Charles Frederick Collins isn't Whitey anymore. He's Rip now. And at 71, he has come full circle.

In those boyhood days, Rip used to walk out of the park with Greenberg. "Hank got to know my grandmother," Rip said. "He'd walk all the way to our house and then take a cab home. Sometimes, he'd sit and talk with my grandmother. She was the first one to call him 'Hankus Pankus.'"

Greenberg gave young Whitey his first baseman's mitt. Fifty years later, when Hank returned for ceremonies to retire his uniform, he autographed the mitt.

Hank helped Collins get a job as visitors batboy and clubhouse man. He had it from 1933 to '36. He knew the day's diamond idols — Babe Ruth, Lou Gehrig, Jimmie Foxx and Lefty Grove.

"Funny thing about the Babe," he recalled. "He wouldn't autograph anything but a baseball. He was always suspicious of someone forging his signature on a letter or contract."

Collins enlisted in the Marines. He went to boot camp at Parris Island, S.C., and later sailed the North Atlantic as an admiral's orderly. Rip requested transfer to Air Naval Training at Chapel Hill, N.C. From there he went to Pensacola, Fla., to become a flight instructor. He used his old Hank Greenberg mitt and played first base on the same Marines team with Ted Williams, who gave him his nickname, Rip.

After the war, Collins was a Detroit fireman for six years. He re-enlisted for the Korean War. As a fighter pilot, he flew 109 missions and won two Distinguished Flying Crosses and eight Air Medals.

On his return to civilian life, Collins became assistant to LeRoy (Friday) Macklem, the Lions' equipment manager. He switched to head equipment man for the Detroit Wheels of the World Football League. When they folded after one season, Rip landed his job as visitors clubhouse man.

Watching modern stars, Collins isn't impressed. He has seen the Babe and Gehrig, so the current millionaires are just customers. In Korea, he watched men die and he knows what a real hero is.

What does impress Rip is warmth, generosity and friendship. He has seen Dwight Evans send his wife to tend to teammate Fred Lynn's ailing wife. He has watched the Angels' Frank Tanana befriend a rookie who was insulted and abused by veteran players.

Collins works long hours — sometimes 14 to 16 a day. But he has a loyal staff: Marty Vagvolgyi, Myron Thomas, Joe Carubb, Willie Mazzone, Dick Mazur and Marcus Collins. Marcus is a third-generation clubhouse man — Rip's grandson. Rip's sons — Bob, Pat and Jim — also worked for him. Jim is a successful plumber now. Bob is a missile technician third class on the USS Will Rogers. Pat is a Marine sergeant who served during Desert Storm.

The young clubhouse boy, Whitey Collins, has come a long way. And the family of Rip Collins carries on that tradition of excellence.

Originally printed on July 20, 1991.

I Was Traded for a Minor League Catcher

Comerica: Love at first sight on Opening Day?

My first look at Comerica Park will come when I sit at the microphone there on Opening Day.

Most other Detroit baseball people have taken an early peek. Not me. I did participate in the ground-breaking ceremonies, but that was just digging a hole in a parking lot.

The only other time I came near the park was the summer of 1999, when Alan Trammell, Lance Parrish and I enjoyed an early dinner in Windsor.

When we returned through the tunnel, I said, "Let's drive up Woodward and measure the distance from the Detroit River to Comerica Park."

We did. It was a little less than a mile. We drove toward the entrance, took a look, but didn't get out of the car.

However, I've seen 19 other new parks in my broadcasting lifetime. In five of them I've broadcast the first game there.

My first broadcast from a new park was April 15, 1954.

The Baltimore Orioles had begun their modern big-league history with two games in Detroit. They took a train to Baltimore. The players dressed on the train, then paraded through downtown Baltimore to their new home, Memorial Stadium.

When we arrived, workmen were still installing

seats and doing other final touch-ups. The Birds beat the White Sox that afternoon, 3-1.

The next time I helped inaugurate a park was in '65. The Tigers were coming north from spring training and played an exhibition game against the Milwaukee Braves at the new Atlanta park, Atlanta-Fulton County Stadium.

Again, the park wasn't quite ready. The grounds crew was still putting down sod when we reached the stadium.

My next first game featured a rout by the Tigers. On April 18, 1991, the Tigers whipped the White Sox, 16-0, at new Comiskey Park. Frank Tanana was the winner. The Tigers knocked out Jack McDowell early and sent most of the crowd of 42,191 home before the fifth inning.

When Jacobs Field in Cleveland opened April 4, 1994, I was there to broadcast the game on CBS radio. President Bill Clinton threw out the first pitch. The Indians beat the Seattle Mariners in the 11th inning on a single by Wayne Kirby.

St. Petersburg, Fla., was the scene of my fifth first-game broadcast. The newest of the American League teams, the Tampa Bay Devil Rays, opened Tropicana Field on March 31, 1998, against the Tigers.

After Hall of Famers Ted Williams, Stan Musial and Monte Irvin threw out the ceremonial first pitches, the Tigers jumped to an early 11-0 lead and went on to win, 11-6.

Originally printed on April 3, 2000

Reese was a classy boy of summer

When Hall of Famer Pee Wee Reese died, my baseball generation lost a friend and a hero. I'd known Reese from his second year in the big leagues. We rode the trains together, played golf together, were partners on the radio and fellow members of the Hall of Fame Veterans Committee.

He was one of the warmest, friendliest players I've known — the personification of class.

I first met Reese in 1941. He and pal Pete Reiser were coming through Atlanta on a Brooklyn Dodgers exhibition trip that spring. Pee Wee and Pete came to the studios at WSB and appeared on my sports show.

Injuries wrecked Reiser's promising career, but Reese went on to become an All-Star and a Hall of Famer. He was team captain, No. 1, and the true leader of the Boys of Summer.

When I broke in with the Dodgers as an announcer in August 1948, Pee Wee was the first to make me feel at home. I taught his wife, Dottie, how to keep score. He was an avid hearts player. Hearts was our game on those long train rides, and I often slipped him the queen of spades and quickly ducked when he angrily fired his cards at me.

Jackie Robinson was usually in those games. Also Gil Hodges and Billy Cox. That was the entire

Brooklyn infield. All of them are gone now, along with Roy Campanella, Rex Barney and Carl Furillo. Those Dodgers were my first big-league team, and they still have a very special place in my heart.

None was classier than Pee Wee. Later, when I broadcast with the Giants, we still would visit each other. Along with his personal warmth, Reese had a tremendous sense of humor and was very adept with the gentle needle. One of his favorite targets was Giants manager Leo Durocher, his onetime Dodgers skipper. Reese had succeeded Leo at shortstop when Durocher retired as a player.

After Pee Wee's playing days, he went into television and radio. For years he was Dizzy Dean's partner on the Game of the Week. I had the pleasure of working with Pee Wee on the NBC radio broadcast of the 1968 World Series. He was in the booth with me in St. Louis when Jim Northrup's triple off Bob Gibson in Game 7 drove in two runs and sent the Tigers to the championship.

Just a few years ago, Reese joined me on the Hall of Fame Veterans Committee. The last time I saw him, Lulu and I had dinner with Pee Wee and Dottie the night before our voting session. He was the same old Pee Wee. Warm, friendly and the epitome of class. Like his friends, I will miss the Captain.

Originally printed on Aug. 20, 1999

Associated Press file photo

Forty years after Bobby Thomson's famous home run, he was reunited with Brooklyn Dodgers pitcher Ralph Branca, who jokingly tried to choke him.

National Baseball Library

Even though there's no record of it, I broadcast Thomson's "Shot Heard 'Round the World" in 1951 on NBC-TV. Thomson's homer in the ninth gave the Giants reason to celebrate and the pennant.

Calling Thomson's shot is a long-gone memory

The home run is the glamour hit of baseball. That fact was reaffirmed in 1998 by the nation's obsession with the Mark McGwire-Sammy Sosa duel.

I've seen a few homers, from Dusty Rhodes' puny poke in the 1954 World Series to McGwire's massive mash over Tiger Stadium's leftfield roof in 1997.

Let's zero in on three home run feats I was lucky enough to broadcast.

The first was Bobby Thomson's "Shot Heard 'Round the World" Oct. 3, 1951. As the New York Giants' announcers, Russ Hodges and I alternated between radio and television. For the final game of the Dodgers-Giants playoffs, it was my turn on television.

"What a break for me," I told myself. "There are five different radio broadcasts, but I'll be alone on NBC-TV, for the first-ever, sponsored coast-to-coast telecast of a sports event."

A fan in New Jersey taped Hodges' radio call of Thomson's home run and mailed the tape to Russ. Our sponsor, Chesterfield cigarettes, issued a recording on which Hodges could be heard repeating: "The Giants win the pennant!" It became the most famous sound bite in sports history.

In those pre-replay days, television did no taping. There was no record of my call of Thomson's home

145

run. Only Mrs. Harwell and I know I telecast that epic home run.

Another missed-tape story happened when I was the radio-TV voice of the Baltimore Orioles. On June 10, 1959, at Memorial Stadium, Cleveland's Rocky Colavito, who later became a Tiger, hit four home runs in one game.

After Rocky's third homer, I said to our producer in the radio booth, "Call the studio and make sure they're ready to tape Colavito's next at-bat. If he hits his fourth home run, I'll have a tape to give Rocky."

Sure enough, the next time up Colavito deposited his fourth homer into the leftfield seats.

"Did the studio tape it?" I asked our producer.

"Oh, I forgot to tell them," he said, wincing.

But I did get a tape of another famous home run. This one was Bucky Dent's blow that beat Boston in the 1978 American League playoff game at Fenway Park. I was at the CBS radio mike when Dent lifted Mike Torrez's pitch just over the Green Monster, into the screen and sent the Yankees to the ALCS against Kansas City. That dinky home run would have been a simple out in any other park.

I gave Dent a copy of the tape.

"On my broadcast," I told him, "I say it's a short fly to left — in for a home run. I hope you don't mind."

"Are you kidding?" he answered. "That's exactly what it was."

Yes, short or long, the home run is still the glamour hit of baseball.

Originally printed on April 5, 1999

Ernie Harwell Collection

Together with Paul Carey, the best voice I ever worked with and my partner for 17 years on Detroit Tigers broadcasts. I miss Paul and all those other great voices.

The days of great voices are history

When radio began in the mid-1920s, voice was everything. That's not true anymore. The voice on radio — and its big brother, TV — is secondary to content. I think the modern way is better, but I miss some of the great voices of the past.

The first announcers came to radio from the ranks of singers. Graham McNamee, pioneer sports announcer, took an audition at NBC as a singer and was soon converted to announcing. He and his early rival, Ted Husing, had fantastic voices. Their vocal coloration enhanced every event they covered.

Later, Bill Stern hit the network sports broadcasting scene. Stern entered radio from the stage. He had been stage manager at RCA Music Hall in New York. His voice had a touch of the dramatic and spawned many imitators in his day.

Despite his great popularity, Stern had a weakness. He knew little about sports, but his lack of knowledge didn't faze him. I broadcast the Masters golf tournament with him for two years, 1942 and 1946, and he insisted on talking about the golfers' points instead of strokes. Certainly a basic faux pas.

Husing was different. To his great voice, he added knowledge and dedication.

Ted was the first announcer who really studied his sport. He gathered background of the event he covered and always displayed a thorough preparation.

Red Barber was the first baseball announcer to take the Husing approach and prepare himself before a game. But Red did not have a great voice. When I worked with him in Brooklyn in 1948-49, his voice was so light and weak that our engineer had to turn up the volume full force.

Today's announcers are much better prepared than the old-timers. The moderns work harder, too, but the emphasis on voice is history. Even the studio announcers — with some exceptions — can't match the great voices of Paul Douglas, Andre Baruch and Don Wilson.

And what about those distinctive news voices? Voices like those of Lowell Thomas, Douglas Edwards, Edward R. Murrow, Gabriel Heatter and Walter Cronkite. They were classic.

Ray Scott had a great sports voice. His Green Bay Packers broadcasts are still remembered. Of the network moderns, Jon Miller and Bob Costas have a fine sound for play-by-play. Most of the analysts don't worry about voice. The content of what they say is much more important than how they say it.

The best voice I ever worked with belonged to Paul Carey, my partner for 17 years on Tigers broadcasts. Everybody loved that deep, booming sound. And along with his voice, Paul brought dedication and thorough preparation.

I miss Paul. And all those other great voices that used to be such an integral part of radio and TV.

Originally printed on April 10, 1998

Barney bled Dodger Blue

It always seemed like the same scenario whenever I visited Rex Barney at his public address microphone in Baltimore.

He'd be talking with an attractive, twentysomething lady.

"Hi, Ernie," he'd say. "Tell this young lady I'm not lying to her — I did pitch a no-hitter."

"Yes, you did," I'd say. "It was Sept. 9, 1948, against the Giants at the Polo Grounds."

"You see," Rex would tell the lady. "He was there. In fact, that was Ernie's first broadcast of a big-league no-hitter. Now do you believe?"

The woman would nod. Rex would put his arm around my shoulder and say to her: "I sorta broke Ernie in. I was the winning pitcher in the first major league game he ever broadcast. Right, Ernie?"

"Right, Rex," I'd answer. "That was about a month before your no-hitter. You beat the Cubs at Ebbets Field, Aug. 4, 1948."

Most Baltimore fans knew Rex Barney as their PA announcer with his signature phrases "Thank Yooooo" and "Give that fan a contract." I knew him as a Dodger.

Rex was proud of his Dodgers heritage. He bled Dodger Blue with an enthusiastic intensity that matched even that of Tommy Lasorda's.

Often after a game we'd have dinner together, and his favorite topics centered around those fabled Boys of Summer — Pee Wee Reese, Jackie

Robinson, Carl Furillo, et al.

He loved those teammates and his years with them. He was never a great pitcher; his wildness robbed him of stardom. Somebody once wrote, "Barney would be in Cooperstown if the plate were high and outside."

Though greatness eluded him, he was still a part of Dodgers lore. That was Barney's proudest accomplishment.

When Rex died, I lost a true friend.

Originally printed on Aug. 15, 1997

Kuralt was on the road with baseball at age 14

Of all the radio-TV stars I've known, the warmest and most down-to-earth was Charles Kuralt — on and off the air. I knew him both ways, as a dinner companion at Hy's in Toronto and as a guest on his Sunday morning CBS-TV show.

Few people know that Kuralt began his famous "On the Road" career as a sports writer.

At the age of 13, in Charlotte, N.C., he entered an essay contest conducted by the Charlotte News. He wrote an essay about his devotion to the Charlotte Hornets baseball team and finished second in the contest. The next year he entered again — again finishing second. This time the judges decided that such a persistent and talented 14-year-old should be rewarded. His prize was to travel on the bus with the Hornets to Knoxville, Tenn., and Asheville, N.C.

Kuralt was ecstatic. He would be riding with his heroes. Also, he would write a story on each game for the News.

Here was this 14-year-old (who had never been away from home) riding into the night with a bunch of hard-bitten, veteran ballplayers. There were a few rookies, but even the youngest was five years older than Kuralt. Charles would write his story, ride the bus to the next town and file his story at the Western Union office.

His editor, Ray Howell, told him to tell the Western Union clerk that he wanted to send his story press rate collect. Kuralt said that was the thrill of his boyhood — going into a Western Union office, throwing out his chest and saying, "Press rate collect."

Through his articles, Kuralt became somewhat of a celebrity. The radio station hired the 14-year-old to do color on the home Hornets broadcasts. He could not drive, so his dad would drop him at the ballpark, listen to the radio and return for him after the game. That was Kuralt's debut on the radio.

He became internationally famous in radio and TV. His best-known show was "On the Road with Charles Kuralt." But remember, he first went on the road and first went on the radio as a 14-year-old baseball expert with the Charlotte Hornets.

Originally printed on July 12, 1997

Ernie Harwell

Keeler will always
be an ace to me

When I was breaking into the sports business, O.B. (Pop) Keeler of the Atlanta Journal was golf's most respected writer. He reached out to me when I needed help and was a profound influence on my career.

Pop was internationally famous. He had covered golf all over the world and trailed the great Bobby Jones in each of his golf adventures.

Keeler was also the author of several best-sellers. When Jones went to Hollywood to appear in films, he took Pop with him to write his scripts and be his chief adviser.

Keeler was Mr. Big, and he was my hero.

In the spring of 1942 I was a young sports announcer at WSB, Atlanta. NBC in New York called and asked me to broadcast the Masters coast-to-coast with Bill Stern. Stern was the nation's top sports announcer, that era's combination of Howard Cosell, Curt Gowdy and Dick Enberg.

This was a great opportunity for me, but I was scared. I played golf; I knew a little about it. However, I was certainly no expert and didn't deserve the Masters assignment.

I called on my hero. I went to O.B. Keeler's home. He warmly welcomed me and introduced me to Mrs. Keeler, better known as Mom. Mom was a golf writer, too, another real expert in the house. All the

154

time O.B. and I chatted about my assignment, Mom was silently knitting in the corner.

Finally, she interrupted.

"O.B.," she said. "I don't understand. Do you mean to tell me that NBC, the number one national network, is broadcasting this big golf event — the Masters — and they're using a young boy just out of school with no experience? He knows absolutely nothing about golf, and he's never broadcast a tournament in his life. I don't believe it."

I felt like crawling under the rug.

"Mom," O.B. said. "Don't worry about it."

He turned to me and put his hand on my knee.

"Son," he said. "Can you count to five?"

"Yes sir." I answered.

"You'll have no trouble broadcasting the Masters. You'll do fine."

That was my first golf broadcast, and now — more than 50 years later — Pop Keeler is still my hero.

Originally printed on Aug. 14, 1996

Enberg prospered despite my advice

I sn't it amazing how friendships sometimes develop?

In the early 1960s, I got a phone call in my room at Los Angeles' Ambassador Hotel.

"My name is Dick Enberg," the caller said. "I'm from Michigan, and I'm a teacher at Northridge College. Could I drop by and say hello?"

My answer was yes. Dick came by, and we went out for an early dinner. Then I invited him to sit in our radio booth and watch the Tigers-Angels game. I discovered that he was from Armada, Mich., and had attended Central Michigan University, where he had worked on the radio.

"I can do a better job than a lot of the announcers I hear today," he told me. "I'm teaching now and helping coach our Northridge baseball team, but I still believe I can be a competent announcer."

His words proved prophetic. Within a few years, he had graduated from TV boxing and wrestling to become the TV voice of the Los Angeles Rams.

Meanwhile, Dick and I developed a friendship through the years. Later at a Los Angeles sports-casters' luncheon, Dick called me aside.

"I've got a chance to be the Angels' announcer," he told me. "But I'm not sure I want to try it. With football, I haven't been away from home very much, but the baseball schedule demands a lot of traveling.

I have a good marriage, and I don't know what effect travel might have on it."

"I wouldn't worry about travel," I told him. "A good marriage can certainly withstand those difficulties."

"Do you think I should take the Angel job?" he asked.

"I do," I told him. "Doing baseball day-to-day will be a great showcase for you. And it can lead to all kinds of success."

Dick took the Angels job and was an immediate success. His marriage was less successful; it had ended in divorce before his first baseball season was over. So much for my marital advice!

But now Enberg is remarried and has gone on to become a premier network voice. He has broadcast outstanding sports events all over the world for NBC-TV and is regarded as one of the best in his profession.

I don't get to see him as much as I used to. But I remember those good dinner conversations in Los Angeles, and Dick sitting in the booth during our Tigers broadcast.

He is a great announcer and deserves all the honors that have come his way. And next time, Dick, I'll do better with my advice on marriage.

Originally printed on June 27, 1996

Early exits were Rizzuto's style

I miss Phil Rizzuto. The little shortstop-turned-broadcaster gave up his microphone when his TV station refused to let him miss a game for Mickey Mantle's funeral.

It was an ironic end to Phil's TV career because he has missed many games — or left early — without any reason and nobody said anything. One of Phil's most famous early departures happened at Tiger Stadium. The Tigers and Yankees battled for 22 innings on June 24, 1962. The Yankees won, 9-7, when outfielder Jack Reed hit the only home run of his three-year career. He hit it off Phil Regan, ending the seven-hour marathon.

After the sixth inning, Rizzuto said good-bye to partner Mel Allen and headed for the airport. "I caught my plane to New York," Rizzuto said. "I landed and hopped into my car. When I turned on our broadcast, I was surprised to hear Mel still broadcasting the game. As I pulled into my driveway in New Jersey, the game still wasn't over."

Rizzuto had moved into the broadcast booth after a Hall of Fame career as the Yankees' shortstop. His best year was 1950, when he batted a career-high .324 and was American League MVP.

After his final season, 1956, he moved directly into the broadcast booth. He quickly learned the secret that made his radio-TV career outstanding:

He learned to be himself. He never posed as an expert or a polished announcer. He was just Phil Rizzuto. He talked about his favorite restaurants and birthdays more than he did the hit-and-run, RBIs or ERA.

"He's a huckleberry," was his mild put-down. And his "Holy Cow!" punctuated many a Yankees highlight play.

After looking at the entry "WW" on Rizzuto's scorecard, one of his friends asked him what it meant.

"WW means wasn't watching" Rizzuto said.

When Rizzuto came to Detroit with the Yankees, he often appeared on the WJR morning show with J.P. McCarthy. However, he couldn't remember McCarthy's initials.

"Is it J.P. or P.J.?" Rizzuto would ask me. I would tell him the correct initials. But when he came in on the next trip, I would ask him, "Phil, have you talked yet with P.J. McCarthy?" After that, he'd be completely confused.

I regret we don't have Scooter to kid around with anymore.

Originally printed on Sept. 2, 1995

Mom happy; son scooped

Sports writers have always chased the elusive "scoop." Sometimes they land that exclusive story; sometimes they miss it.

This is about a miss. It's a story told to me by the man who made the miss, Harold Parrott. Harold was the first big-league traveling secretary I knew. I traveled with him when I broke in with the Brooklyn Dodgers in 1948. Not only was he competent in his job, but he had been an outstanding sports writer.

Yet he missed a scoop on Casey Stengel getting the Dodgers' manager job.

In the early 1930s, Parrott was a boy genius, covering sports for the Brooklyn Eagle. All of sudden he found himself appointed to cover the Dodgers' spring training in Miami. There was one drawback. Harold was still living with his mother, who ruled his life with an iron hand. Mother didn't want son Harold to go to Miami and live with those sunburned sinners along the beach.

Parrott enlisted the help of two sports writers — Tom Meany of the New York Telegram and Bill McCullough of the Brooklyn Times. Both telephoned Harold's mother and told her that they would watch over him. Besides, they added, all the baseball writers were so busy they never had a chance to drink or carouse.

McCullough also promised that his wife Gladys would see that no evil befell Mrs. Parrott's young son.

Gladys McCullough did keep an eye out for Harold. She came looking for him every evening about 6 o'clock because her husband, Bill, was too drunk to write his story. So Harold had to write not only his own story but also one for the incapacitated McCullough.

The big story that spring revolved around the Dodgers' manager. Max Carey was soon to be fired. There was much speculation about his successor. McCullough was drinking heavily and couldn't write his stories. Parrott continued to cover for him. Branch Rickey, then with the Cards, talked McCullough into a pledge to quit drinking.

A week later, Rickey revisited the Dodgers camp.

"Bill isn't drinking anymore?" he asked hopefully.

"No, Mr. Rickey," Gladys answered. "But not any less, either."

Big names were being mentioned as the new Dodgers manager. Parrott would give one the inside track when he wrote his story for the Eagle. Later that night when he ghosted for McCullough, he would name some different manager for the Brooklyn Times.

Early one morning while still sober, McCullough received a postcard from Glendale, Calif. The message was: "Leaving for Brooklyn on business." It was signed Casey Stengel. Bill didn't show the postcard to Parrott, and Harold thought it odd that McCullough wrote his own story that night for the first time in more than a week.

McCullough broke the story that Stengel would be named the new Brooklyn manager within a day or two.

He scooped the other 11 Dodgers reporters — including Parrott, who had written most of his stories all spring. It was one of the few stories he wrote all spring, but it was the biggest one of the year in the chronicle of the Dodgers.

Parrott missed the scoop because the man he had befriended finally turned out a story of his own.

Originally printed on Aug. 7, 1992

Ernie Harwell Collection

As a boy, I first heard baseball on the radio in 1926. My older brother, Davis, and I shared a pair of earphones and listened to the seventh game of the World Series. From then on I was hooked.

Baseball and radio: A perfect pair

B aseball and radio have coexisted for more than 70 years. Before these two American institutions merged, fans had only newspapers to depend on for news about their diamond heroes.

Television emerged in the late '40s and now has taken a dominant position. But there will always be a place for radio and baseball to be together.

My first radio-baseball memory goes back to the 1926 World Series. My older brother, Davis, had a crystal set in our basement in Atlanta. With great pride he would move the little piece of wire called a cat whisker over a dab of mercury and pull in a station from Pittsburgh or some farther city. There wasn't a loudspeaker — only a pair of earphones. Davis would put one of the phones over his ear and give me the other one. I heard that famous seventh game of the '26 World Series when Grover Cleveland Alexander fanned Tony Lazzeri and the Cards went on to beat the Yankees.

From then on I was hooked on radio. In a few years, local stations began to broadcast the Atlanta Crackers' games. Our family didn't have a radio then, and I would walk through the neighborhood until I heard the baseball broadcast coming through a window. Then I would camp under that window as long as I could without arousing the suspicions of the household.

The Atlanta announcers didn't travel with the Crackers. When the team was on the road they recreated the game in a studio. This lasted in the minors for many years and is still done in some markets. The major league announcers gave up re-creating in the early 1950s.

The Midwest was far ahead of the Eastern cities in baseball broadcasting. On Aug. 5, 1921, Harold Arlin broadcast the first baseball game ever on radio. By the late '20s, Detroit, Chicago and other cities were covering their teams on a regular basis. Ty Tyson in Detroit had been on the air 11 years before any of the New York clubs aired their games. The Yankees, Dodgers and Giants had a pact in which they agreed not to broadcast because they felt it would hurt attendance.

After Larry MacPhail took over the Dodgers, he broke that agreement in 1939.

Now broadcasting is a big item everywhere. Despite the popularity of TV, radio lives on in cars, on beaches, in shops and homes. In the late '40s there were 16 teams in the two big leagues. Each team had one — sometimes two — announcers. Now there are 26 big-league teams. Each radio broadcast has two or three announcers. Cable has two or three; and the commercial TV stations bring another two or three.

I think the modern announcers are better informed and harder workers than the old-timers. Maybe not as colorful, but they have to be better because the audience today is so much better informed than the fans were in the late '40s.

Baseball and radio has been a great association. And it will continue to be for a long time.

Originally printed on May 15, 1992

Still in the booth, 43 years later

A ug. 4 might not mean a lot to you, but it was a significant date in my career. On the night of Aug. 4, 1948, I broadcast my first big-league game.

It was a time I thought would never come. And when it did, it was delayed 24 hours by rain.

My ambition had always been to be a big-league announcer. After eight years in radio — interrupted by four years in the Marines — I was in Brooklyn to broadcast a Cubs-Dodgers game from Ebbets Field over radio station WMCA.

In the past were years of broadcasting Atlanta Crackers minor league games. Years of compiling our statistics while riding the streetcar after night games. Years of working alone, doing telegraphic re-creations of the road games. Years of hoping for that big-league chance.

Two events had propelled me to the big leagues. First, Red Barber, the famed Dodgers announcer, had been hospitalized with a bleeding ulcer. Second, his boss, Branch Rickey, had traded a minor league catcher for me. Yes, the man I worked for — Earl Mann, Atlanta Crackers owner — had told Rickey he would allow me to go to Brooklyn only if Rickey would send Atlanta its Montreal catcher, Cliff Dapper.

My first game was to be Tuesday, Aug. 3. I flew to

Brooklyn on Monday and arrived that night at the Bossert Hotel. I had 24 hours to get ready.

I was alone in Brooklyn. I had never seen a National League game. I had seen only one major league game (at Comiskey Park, in 1934). I didn't even know where Ebbets Field was. All I could do was wait.

I waited and waited. Late Tuesday afternoon I learned my first broadcast would be delayed another 24 hours because that night's game with the Cubs had been rained out. More waiting. I was very nervous.

It was still raining on Wednesday morning. I waited and hoped. Finally the skies cleared. I caught a subway to Ebbets Field. What a thrill when I walked into that historic little ballpark. All my life I'd read about it. Now I was there.

I met my broadcast partner, Connie Desmond. He was warm and friendly and introduced me to the Dodgers. They accepted me right away. I was now with the fabled Boys of Summer — Jackie Robinson, Pee Wee Reese, Duke Snider, Preacher Roe and Gil Hodges.

"Hey, Ernie!" It was Russ Meyer, the Cubs' pitcher.

I had known Meyer when he pitched for Nashville in the Southern League. His greeting relaxed me. I realized that here in this strange park, trying to do a strange job, I had found a friend.

Less than an hour later, Meyer was at the center of one of those famed Brooklyn rhubarbs. Robinson stole home in the first inning. Meyer began to rave and rant at Jackie and at umpire Frank Dascoli. Some of his profane remarks were picked up by our field mike. Meyer was ejected from the game by Dascoli and later fined $150.

I don't remember much else about that game. I was nervous and excited. I do recall that the Dodgers won, 5-4, scoring the winning run in the last half of the ninth inning. Rex Barney was the winner and the loser in relief was Bob (Dutch) McCall.

Somehow I made it through that first broadcast. It took awhile for the excitement to subside. I caught a streetcar and got back safely to the Bossert Hotel. I was now a big-league announcer.

At the time, Aug. 4, 1948, I didn't know how long I'd stay around.

I'm still here.

Originally printed on Aug. 3, 1991

Ernie Harwell Collection

Not every radio announcer needs a signature call, and the calls certainly shouldn't be contrived. Most of my trademark phrases — such as "Long Gone!" — came to me late in my career on a whim.

It's a calling; don't force it

D oes a baseball announcer need signature
phrases — trademarks by which his listeners
identify him?

I don't think so. Granted, Mel Allen's "How about
that?" and Russ Hodges' "Bye Bye, Baby" were
famous and made them distinctive. But there are
top-notch announcers today who have no special
home run calls or identifying phrases. Vin Scully
and Jon Miller, to name a couple.

So if those phrases come naturally, that's fine. But
if they are contrived, they don't work. I've seen
young announcers struggle to develop a trademark
call — especially for the home run. My advice:
Forget it, unless it just happens for you. Trying too
hard ruins it all.

Most of my special phrases came late in my
career. The exception was, "He stood there like the
house by the side of the road." I began using this
phrase just after I started broadcasting Atlanta
Crackers games in 1946. It comes from a poem, "The
House By the Side of the Road," by Sam Walter
Foss.

Homer once wrote: "He was a friend to man, and
he lived in a house by the side of the road." Foss
turned around that phrase and ended the fifth and
final verse of his poem with, "Let me live in my
house by the side of the road and be a friend to
man."

I recited Foss' poem when I was in the fifth grade

in Atlanta.

My "Long Gone!" call didn't happen until the 1980s, and it came by accident. A batter hit a long drive, and I said: "It's long, it's long, it's long gone." Now I say it for almost every home run.

"Two for the price of one" came about the same way. I don't even remember when I said it for the first time — probably sometime in the 1970s.

The gimmick about the foul balls into the seats started right after I came to Detroit. A batter sliced a foul into the seats behind first base. Just off the cuff, I said something like: "A man from Saginaw will be taking that one home." After that, as I walked through the stands, people would ask: "How 'bout letting a guy from Dearborn (or some other locality) catch one tonight?" And so it grew.

"Instant runs" just crept up on me by accident, too. I first used that phrase sometime in the mid-1960s. I can't even recall when I started my other signature phrases. I never sat down to develop them.

Certainly they are not necessary. Some fans like them; others don't. You just have to be natural and let fans take their choice.

Originally printed on June 5, 1998

Purely
Personal

Some of my favorite things

This is purely personal.

If I had a life to live again, I would: Learn to be a handyman. ... Eat more ice cream and less bran. ... Read more of the Bible and less modern fiction. ... Get to know the hotel managers. ... Do more sightseeing when I travel. ... Walk in the woods more often. ... Try to be kind instead of correct.

I might be crazy, but I like a lot of foods others can't stand. My list includes okra, figs, prunes, grits, broccoli, spinach and grapefruit. My favorite food is corn bread. Corn on the cob is a close second. My least favorite food is liver.

I like: dogs and cats, quiet dinners, sunrises, radios, popcorn, movies, good conversation, softspoken ladies, kids with baseball gloves, Thanasis Restaurant in Windsor, walking into a baseball stadium and seeing the green grass and bright sunshine, letters from old schoolmates or friends from my years in the Marines, baseball in the daytime, a smile and a kind word.

I don't like: stamp machines, pushy autograph seekers, plastic packages wrapped too tightly, artificial turf, bad grammar, people who can't get past "the good old days," newspaper coin boxes, rain delays, fried food, people who don't identify themselves on the phone ... and those who give you only their first name, self-serve gas pumps, intricate telephone-answering systems with no human voices,

pre-sectioned grapefruit, media overkill, lumpy oat-
meal, long-winded speakers, people who end state-
ments with "OK?", ethnic jokes, committee meetings, highway construction and detours, envelopes
that won't stick.

Here are some of my favorites:

Big-league city — Milwaukee; hotel — Pfister in
Milwaukee; on-the-road restaurant — Hausner's in
Baltimore; ballpark — three-way tie among Coors
Field, Camden Yards and Jacobs Field; tree — dog-
wood; flower — rose; writer — John Updike; pop
singer — Nat King Cole; movie — "My Cousin
Vinny"; song — "Vincent."

Originally printed on July 9, 1998

And now, the one and onlys

I t takes the onlys of life to add sparkle to our existence. For instance: the only girl you ever loved; the only friend who defended you; the only teacher who thought you might be a success.

Here are some of my onlys during my journey through baseball.

Only player to ask to sit in the radio booth and hear me broadcast: George Brett.

Only player to ask me to review his speech when he was honored in pregame ceremonies: Ted Williams.

Only umpire to let me rub up baseballs before a regular American League game: Jim Evans.

Only manager to cry when I spoke in Baseball Chapel: John McNamara.

Only ex-sports announcer to invite me to lunch at the White House: President Ronald Reagan.

Only player I was traded for: Cliff Dapper.

Only player to deliver a message to my radio booth while in uniform: Eddie Murray.

Only player to rent me his home: Jim Essian.

Only coach to rent my home: Jimy Williams.

Only player whose wife furnished me with her spaghetti sauce: Sal Maglie.

Only player to give me stock in his paint company: Denny McLain.

Only manager to fight with me: Leo Durocher.

Only anthem singer to sing a Harwell-written song in duet with me: Robert Merrill.

Only executive to chastise me for erroneously "postponing" a game on my broadcast: Jim Campbell.

Only executive to fly me to spring training in his private plane: Branch Rickey.

Only manager whose movie star wife interviewed me on TV: Durocher.

Only anthem singer who sang "Georgia on My Mind" in duet with me at a Detroit charity luncheon: Pearl Bailey.

Only player to co-host a cruise with me: Jim Northrup.

Only manager who let me take pregame practice with his team: Burt Shotton.

Only anthem singer who let me select his wife: Jose Feliciano.

Only player whose wife I taught to score a game: Pee Wee Reese.

Only player to induct me into the Baseball Hall of Fame: Ralph Kiner.

Only player to shop for my wedding gift the day before he pitched a World Series game: Whitlow Wyatt.

Only player who became a movie director and cast me in his film: Ron Shelton.

Originally printed on June 20, 1997

These odds and ends are odd to no end

Maybe you knew these baseball odds and ends, maybe not:

• The great manager, John McGraw, was such a tyrant in his early career that none of the New York writers — or anybody else — could interview him. McGraw wrote his own reports and handed them to Bozeman Bulger, one of the writers. Bulger then passed the reports to other writers.

In McGraw's day, the games began at 3:30. McGraw demanded that his players sign into the clubhouse before 10 a.m. An alarm went off at 10; if a player was not there, watch out!

• Most baseball historians credit the start of slow-ball pitching (or the change-up) to Herman (Ham) Iburg. He launched the "nothing pitch" while with the Phillies in 1902.

• During a season, the difference in hitting .300 or .248 is only one hit per week. Figure this way: Get 150 hits in 500 at-bats, and your average is 300. If you get only 124 hits in 500 times, your average drops to .248. A season usually lasts 26 weeks. So one hit per week makes a lot of difference.

• Babe Ruth is famous for switching from pitching to becoming a position player. Other well-knowns did it the other way. Some who went from position players to pitcher were Bob Lemon, Bucky Walters, Bob Smith and Hal Jeffcoat.

● There once was a baseball game devoid of cheering, booing or any kind of noise. Because of an anti-Sunday law in New Jersey, when the Giants played at Jersey City on Sunday, April 19, 1919, the clubs asked patrons to refrain from making any kind of noise.

● When Kansas City had a team in the National League in the 1880s, the club posted a sign on the grandstand wall that read: "Please do not shoot the umpire. He is doing the best he can."

● Baseball rules today say that a runner can tag a base and run as soon as the fly ball touches a fielder's glove. It was not always that way. In the late 1800s, a runner could not leave his base until the fielder had held the ball for a catch.

But Tommy McCarthy, an outfielder for the Boston Braves, caused a rule change. Tommy's trick was to keep juggling the ball before he caught it. He would run all the way into the infield and keep the runner from advancing.

● Gene Mauch retired as a player in true hang-'em-up fashion. He had begun to manage Minnesota when that team was in the minors. But he also continued to play. After a 2-for-56 slump, Gene asked the clubhouse attendant for a hammer and nails. He nailed his baseball shoes into the wall behind his locker.

● Leo Durocher quit as a player in 1945. His retirement was prompted when super-slow Ernie Lombardi beat out an infield hit to Leo at shortstop.

● Walter Johnson pitched 369⅔ innings in 1916 for Washington and did not allow a home run. That's a major league record. The National League mark is held by Vic Willis of Pittsburgh. In 1906, he allowed no home runs in 322 innings.

Originally printed on Sept. 6, 1996

Ernie Harwell

Bet you didn't know all this

D on't say I didn't tell you:
For many years, Sunday baseball was banned in major league cities. The Cleveland Indians in 1902-03 played Sunday games in Canton, Columbus and Dayton, Ohio, and Ft. Wayne, Ind. The Tigers transferred Sunday games to Columbus, Toledo and Grand Rapids. ... When Giants pitcher William VanLandingham debuted in 1994, he became the 13th player in major league baseball with 13 letters in his last name. The last 13-letter man was Kirk Dressendorfer in 1991. ... The Tigers had a 13-letter player in their early American League days: outfielder Lou Schiappacasse (1902).

The New York Yankees became the first major league team to retire a number when they retired Lou Gehrig's No. 4 in 1939. ... A major leaguer's first at-bat is never to be forgotten, but here's a strange one. In Dwight Evans' batting debut — on Sept. 16, 1972 — he batted out of turn, popping to Cleveland Indians shortstop Frank Duffy. ...

The first time a public address system was used in the major leagues was Aug. 25, 1929, at the Polo Grounds in New York. The announcer? Umpire Cy Rigler, working with a microphone in his mask. ... In 1919, Babe Ruth hit 29 home runs; the other members of the Boston Red Sox totaled four. ...

Ted Williams once told me that the hardest-throwing pitcher he ever faced was Steve Dalkowski, who toiled in the Orioles' system but never made the big leagues. Steve's fastball once broke an umpire's mask and another time ripped off a batter's ear. In nine years, Dalkowski averaged 13 walks and 13 strikeouts per nine innings. ... Life span for a new ball in major league play is only five pitches. ... The American League adopted the one-visit-to-the-mound rule in the late 1950s because of Paul Richards, who was always overextending his welcome at the mound. ... Baseball's first double-header was played in Baltimore on Oct. 4, 1884, against Indianapolis. Admission: 25 cents. ...

The Tigers' first home night game did not start until 9:30. Officials thought they should wait until complete darkness. ... The White Sox hit only three home runs in 156 games in 1908. ... Mickey Lolich, not in the Hall of Fame, won 10 more games lifetime than Tigers Hall of Famer Hal Newhouser. Lolich won 217. ...

Gavvy Cravath, the home-run record holder until Ruth came along, was a late bloomer. He did not become a major league starter until he was 31, but led the National League in home runs for six of his first seven years. He won his final championship in 1919 at age 38. ...

The sporting goods people can get eight gloves out of a steer. ... The first major leaguer to wear sunglasses was Fred Clarke of the Pirates. ... Ruth was once arrested for violating child-labor laws. His crime was bringing kids on stage, talking to them and giving them autographed balls. Charges eventually were dropped. ...

When Hall of Famer Frankie Frisch first reported

to the New York Giants, he batted crosshanded. . . . How's this for improvement? Atlanta's Ron Gant batted .177 in 1989 and jumped to .303 the next season. . . . There have been five sets of twins in major league history. . . . Cecil Fielder set a record with 76 home runs in his first 1,000 at-bats.

Originally printed on May 12, 1995

Aficionados differ on their favorite kind of game

What kind of baseball game do you like best? I put this question to many people. Their answers:

FRANK THOMAS, White Sox slugger: "I like a medium-type game with a score something like 6-5. That game will have some interesting flow and a lot of turning points."

SPARKY ANDERSON, Tigers manager: "Give me a game with a lot of hitting and a lot of runscoring."

CURT SMITH, author of "Voices of Baseball": "I prefer a hitting game, something like 10-9. For instance, I loved the last game of the 1960 World Series when the Pirates came back and won the seventh game, 10-9."

PHIL GARNER, Brewers manager: "My favorite game is one filled with possible strategic moves — the kind that usually ends 6-5 or 7-6."

CECIL FIELDER, Tigers slugger: "My choice is a two-hour, 30-minute game with the final score 4-3. I like a game with not too many runs, but not too few, either."

J.P. McCARTHY, WJR morning host: "Give me a game with a lot of runs and a lot of action. Let it finish in under four hours."

TIM FOLI, Brewers coach: "I like a game where one play can be significant. If there is too much scoring, various plays don't stand out."

FRED McLEOD, TV sports anchor: "The game which appeals to me is one in which a lot of strikes are thrown. I like it quick-paced with my team winning, 4-3, in the ninth inning."

GENE LAMONT, White Sox manager: "The best kind of game for me happened in Seattle when our Jack McDowell beat the Mariners' Randy Johnson, 2-1. We had five hits, and Seattle got only three. Also, there were some great plays and the game moved right along."

JIM PRICE, Tigers radio announcer: "Give me a pitching duel every time. My favorite final score is 2-1 or 1-0."

JIM NORTHRUP, former Tigers outfielder: "I like all kinds of games as a spectator. As a player, I'd take a 13-12 game, one in which I got four hits."

BILL WILDERN, longtime Tigers loyalist: "I prefer the classic, close, hard-fought game. My favorite of all time is the Tigers' 4-1 victory over St. Louis in the final game of the 1968 World Series."

JIM HUNTER, CBS Radio: "The best kind of game is one my team wins in the ninth. Almost every pitch means something."

NORM BAER, CBS baseball producer: "The score doesn't matter to me. I just want a game which is crisply played and has some dramatic moments in it."

FRED SMITH, Tigers historian: "I like some hitting in a game, maybe a final score of 8-7, but not a 15-13 game. I enjoy seeing a lot of clutch situations."

PAUL CAREY, my longtime broadcast partner: "I

want to see a game that ends 1-0 in two hours. It should be scoreless until it is decided in the ninth inning."

JOHN LOWE, Detroit Free Press writer: "Two classic playoff games illustrate the game I like best. One was the Bucky Dent 1978 home run in Boston; the other, the Bobby Thomson home run game in 1951. The final score was 5-4 in each game. Those are games in which every runner is a stick of lighted dynamite."

Originally printed on Aug. 19, 1994

Ernie Harwell Collection

Oakland and San Francisco always bring a smile to my face. The Bay Area is a great place to spend an easy, do-nothing day off that might begin with activities that start at 6:25 a.m. and don't end until after 10:30 p.m.

Sometimes, a day off is a day on the run

The Tigers' first scheduled off day arrived the day after the night opener in Oakland, Calif.

Usually, baseball travelers prefer off days at home. But if there's a road off day, Oakland is a good place to have it because across the bay is San Francisco, almost everybody's favorite city.

I made no special plans and anticipated an easy, do-nothing kind of off-day. I scheduled only a dinner with Dick Tracewski at Mulhern and Schachern's, a great San Francisco restaurant owned by a friend. I invited Rick Rizzs and Bob Rathbun to join us. Dick was bringing Gene Roof.

Here is a sketchy timetable of the off-day:

● 6:25 a.m. — Radio station calls for short interview.

● 7:05 a.m. — Breakfast at coffee shop.

● 7:50 a.m. — Read article from Upper Room magazine and passage from Genesis about Abraham and Isaac.

● 8:10 a.m. — Phone Leo Merta, a friend in Half Moon Bay. He accepts dinner invitation. Will pick us up at 5 p.m.

● 8:40 a.m. — Phone home. Lulu tells me John Lowe's game story made the Free Press despite game's late end. We discuss my "Entertainment Tonight" interview and when it might run.

● 8:50 a.m. — Read two chapters of great new

novel "Second Fire" by Robert Wilson, a Tigers fan from Redford.

● 9 a.m. — Phone Scott Nickle in the marketing department at Tiger Stadium. He's in meeting and will call back.

● 9:20 a.m. — Phone Gene Myers at Free Press to discuss column deadline.

● 10:15 a.m. — Rick Rizzs phones. He and Bob might not join us at dinner. They are going to San Francisco early and might not stay that long.

● 11:30 a.m. — Take 25-minute walk to movie theater. Eat banana and apple on the way.

● Noon — Begin watching "Born Yesterday" — alone. Three more people drift in.

● 3 p.m. — Walk back to hotel for 20-minute nap.

● 3:30 p.m. — Do stretching exercises in room and jump rope.

● 3:45 p.m. — Scott Nickle phones and reads off list of play-by-play on Ernie Harwell cassette for Tigers' giveaway.

● 3:50 p.m. — Watch end of Roy Firestone's "Up Close." Mitch Albom is on.

● 4 p.m. — Take warm bath.

● 4:10 p.m. — Dave Newhouse of the Oakland Tribune phones. Has written column about our broadcast and wants a tape.

● 4:25 p.m. — A call from lobby. A young man named Tim from Santa Clara says he is an aspiring announcer and wants to talk with me. He visits my room and we discuss his career possibilities.

● 5 p.m. — We leave for restaurant.

● 5:35 p.m. — We arrive at restaurant.

● 6 p.m. — Talking baseball.

● 7:40 p.m. — Ed Moose, who owns nearby restaurant, joins our group. He's a Cardinals fan.

● 8:20 p.m. — Finish great salmon, return to hotel.

● 8:30 p.m. — Watch baseball on ESPN — Toronto at Seattle.

● 8:45 p.m. — Todd Miller of Mayo Smith Society phones to confirm interview with Rick, Bob and me.

● 9:15 p.m. — Start San Francisco Chronicle crossword puzzle.

● 10:20 p.m. — KMPC of Los Angeles calls; I do interview about the Tigers.

● 10:30 p.m. — Back to crossword puzzle; 71-across asks: "And —" Pepys sign-off.

● 10:31 p.m. — I write in answer: "So to bed."

● 10:33 p.m. — I take hint, and so to bed.

Originally printed on April 9, 1993

Answers to some never-asked questions

H ere are some questions I thought you'd never ask:
Why do managers and coaches in baseball wear uniforms when those in other sports wear street clothes?

Answer: The manager of baseball's first pro team was Harry Wright, a centerfielder.

Naturally, he had to wear a uniform. And baseball managers have worn uniforms ever since.

When did battery signs originate?

Answer: They were first used by Connie Mack when he was catching for Washington in 1888.

What team sponsored the first bat day?

Answer: The St. Louis Browns. In 1952 their business manager, Rudy Schaffer, bought 12,000 bats at a closeout sale and gave them away at a doubleheader. The Browns drew 15,000 for that first bat day.

What event prompted the retirement of Leo Durocher?

Answer: When the slow-footed Ernie Lombardi hit a grounder to Leo at shortstop and beat it out, Leo knew he was through.

It was 1945 and Durocher was 40 years old and had played for 17 years in the major leagues.

What Tiger has children born in three countries?

Answer: Bill Gullickson. Bill became a dad in

Canada, Japan and the United States.

What was Bob Uecker's advice for catching a knuckleball?

Answer: Wait until the ball stops rolling, then pick it up.

What was the quietest game in baseball history?

Answer: A game between the New York Giants and Jersey City in Jersey City on Sunday, April 19, 1919.

Sunday baseball was illegal in Jersey City, so officials insisted that the fans refrain from noisemaking. The game was completely devoid of cheering, booing or any other kind of noise.

What major-leaguer was not pictured on his rookie bubblegum card?

Answer: Aurelio Rodriguez. When the former Tigers third baseman was with California, the Topps photographer mistook the Angels' batboy for Rodriguez and the batboy's picture was printed on Rodriguez's card.

What manager would not allow his team to use the visitors clubhouse in an away World Series game?

Answer: John McGraw.

McGraw hated the New York Yankees so much that he kicked them out of his ballpark, the Polo Grounds.

When the Giants played the Yanks in the 1923 World Series, McGraw refused to let his team use the clubhouse at Yankee Stadium.

To which player did the expression, "Good field, no hit" first apply?

Answer: Mike Gonzales, scouting for the Cardinals, put that label on Moe Berg, who later became a major-leaguer and a World War II spy.

Originally printed on Sept. 18, 1992

How to live on the road

Travel in baseball is very important. It might not have the 80 percent importance rating of pitching, but we all know that travel is 50 percent of baseball.

Two managers, Paul Richards and Earl Weaver, hated to travel. "I enjoy the game and the sense of competition," Richards told me. "But I can't stand the loneliness of a hotel room."

It's no wonder that many players and coaches are at the ballpark as early as 2 p.m. for a 7:30 game.

So this will be about travel. Some observations, hints, proverbs, definitions and questions — all personal, just one man's opinions.

● Proverbs: Never call home; there is sure to be a crisis. ... Never eat at any place called Mom's. ... The higher the altitude of a restaurant, the worse the food. ... Quality of a meal varies inversely with the height of the pepper shaker. ... Never change planes in Chicago or Atlanta.

● Packing hint: Put all your clothes on one bed. Put all your money on another. Reduce the clothes by half and double the amount of money.

● Questions: Do maids and housekeepers take college courses in how to yammer loudly in hotel corridors at 7:30 a.m.? Is there anything dimmer than a hotel room light bulb? Why do airline ticket sellers spend five minutes on a computer when they could write a ticket in half the time? Why are there no real clocks in airports? Who teaches voice training to airline flight attendants?

• Definitions: Catch of the day is whatever the wholesaler offered to the chef as a good deal. ... An airline snack means a pack of 18 salted peanuts.

• Pet peeves: Card keys to hotel rooms. ... You get to your room on the 36th floor, the key doesn't work, and you have to return to the front desk for another. ... The servi-bar in your room. ... Only $8.50 for a small pack of cashews. ... I wonder whether the hotel owners realize what a temptation the bar might be to an alcoholic by himself in a lonely room.

• Travel in the world of literature: Patrick Dennis quoted two observant employees in his novel "Pink Hotel." The Chef: "Thank God for white cream sauce. It can cover any culinary mediocrity." The telephone operator: "If I don't like a guest, I sock him with a few more phone calls on his bill."

• Waiter joke: Customer asks, "Who's gonna win the big game?" Waiter answers, "Sorry, sir, this is not my table."

• Worst travel scenario: "Sorry, but we've canceled your flight." It happened to me last October in Baltimore. I was confirming (I thought) my flight to New York when I heard the bad news. Worst travel scenario No. 2: There's a convention at your hotel. It's the National Association of High School Cheerleaders. No. 3: There is heavy construction outside your window ... the air hammer tunes up at 6:45 a.m.

• More questions: Does anybody ever fill out those suggestion questionnaires? Why do most hotels ignore climatic conditions and set their thermostats according to the calendar? You get heat on a warm winter day and cold air conditioning when it's cool in the spring.

● Hints: Never eat or shoot craps above the ground floor. ... Never trust a guy who wears his jacket off his shoulder. ... To ward off pickpockets, wrap your money with a rubber band. Any dip can get into your pocket, but the rubber band creates friction and the dollar bill can't be removed without your feeling it.

Originally printed on June 26, 1992

Recognize these guys?

When you've been around baseball for a while, you see all sorts of players. They come in different shapes, sizes and temperaments. Most of them fit into one of these categories:

1. BILLY THE BANDAGE: An adhesive-tape worm. Keeps himself on pills and needles. ... First in the whirlpool, first on the rubbing table, last on the field (a rub-tub-sub). ... He has tried every medicine. Next week, embalming fluid. ... Even the look he gives you is a hurt look. Not only are his ailments chronic, they're chronicles. ... Always in the punk of condition.

2. LOVER LOUIE: Never married, but he has had a lot of near Mrs. ... Troubled by curves. ... More effective at night — late at night. Will chase anything but a fly ball.

3. BELLIGERENT BASIL: One half of a fight looking for the other half. He'd climb a mountain to take a punch at an echo. ... Loves a fight so much, he has been married six times.

4. POROUS PAUL: He couldn't stop a grapefruit from rolling uphill. Plays every hop perfectly — except the last one. ... No matter where his manager puts him in the lineup, he can't hide him from the opposition. Leads league in runs-booted-in. ... A holier-than-thou defensive debit.

5. ORVILLE AND OUT: The pitcher's best friend. As a hitter, he has ruined more rallies than tear gas.

. . . Qualifies for trapeze act because his only attributes are a swing and a miss.

6. SLOW FREIGHT FREDDIE: It takes a triple to score him from third. . . . He not only runs like he has a piano on his back, he also stops and plays "God Bless America" on the way. . . . Nickname is E Pluribus Unum because he can't get off a dime.

7. PERCENTAGE PATRICK: His mother must have been frightened by a computer because he is forever figuring. . . . Can't remember whether his team won or lost, but he can tell you his batting average to the final percentage point. . . . Officious with the official scorer.

8. CONCEITED CHARLES: In love with himself — and he has no competition. . . . A case of mistaken nonentity. . . . Suffers from I strain. . . . On his 24th birthday he sent a telegram of congratulations to his mother. . . . Hasn't an enemy in the world, but all his friends hate him.

9. STUFFER SAM: If calories counted in the official averages, he would be leading the league. . . . Way out in front. Always exceeding the feed limit. . . . Far from his old sylph. . . . Sure to get his just desserts.

10. RAVER RALPH: Named year after year as the game's Most Voluble Player. . . . A man who pops off even more than he pops up. Often is thrown out spieling. . . . Mama's little yelper. . . . Approaches every subject with an open mouth. His future is in the radio or TV booth.

11. MONEY MAN MARVIN: Only sign he doesn't miss is the dollar sign. . . . Spends more time with

his agent than with his teammates. ... Doesn't care if the game is on the line — only if his signature is. ... Rather see a pitch from his broker than from a hard-throwing opponent.

Originally printed on April 10, 1992

It's not stretching the truth

There's no sustained thrill in sports that can match a pennant race. Here are some of the things bound to happen down the stretch:

● The managers of the contending clubs will say, "It all depends on pitching."

● Television camera crews will go on the road with the team.

● Each TV station will feature interviews with loud fans in loud bars.

● A rookie reliever will pick up a surprise victory.

● A non-contender will use an unknown pitcher against a contender. The other contenders will protest; the unknown probably will win.

● Radio stations will be flooded with new songs about the team.

● The newspaper will send three more staffers to each game.

● Each paper will issue a special section with profiles of the players.

● Ads to buy and sell tickets will appear in the classifieds.

● More players will do TV and radio commercials.

● The teams' front offices will say: "We're making every effort to strengthen the team, but we're not going to wreck our farm system."

● A key player will suffer a severe injury and miss the rest of the season.

● Sudden rains will create unwanted doubleheaders.

● A player will say, "This is what baseball is all about."

● Another will say, 'Now it's fun to come to the ballpark."

● Bumper stickers saluting the team will spring up all over the city.

● Some fans will be surprised when the ballpark is not sold out for every game down the stretch.

● Disgruntled millionaire players won't understand why the club can't renegotiate their contracts in the final three weeks.

● The magic number suddenly emerges.

● All the dopesters become Iffy, and everybody tries to figure which team has the schedule advantage.

● The team wins three straight and one of the coaches refuses to change his underwear.

● Although losing a game, a team will clinch the division and will be accused of backing in.

● Another team will be accused of choking when it loses two in a row.

● One team will be favored because "it's been through this kind of pressure before."

● Underdog players will say, "We're as good as those high-talented guys because we put our pants on one leg at a time."

Originally printed on Aug. 31, 1991

Count on this, for openers

Opening Day is my favorite day of the year.
It's a glorious combination of Christmas,
Easter and the Fourth of July.

● Christmas: Baseball opening its presents.

● Easter: Baseball's birth of spring with some fans, like churchgoers, showing up for only that one time in the year.

● Fourth of July: Baseball's celebration, a Michigan civic event of sportanic fireworks.

I've seen all kinds of openers — in 80-degree weather and in the snow; tight pitching duels and one-sided fiascos; long, boring games and close, exciting ones.

I've seen enough of them to predict what might happen on a typical Opening Day. Something like:

The first group of fans in the stadium will be the bleacherites. At least six of them — despite near-freezing weather — will not be wearing shirts.

The rookie pitcher for the home team will report late because he couldn't find the ballpark.

The uniforms will be cleaner. The grass will be greener.

Outside the park, radio music from the blaring loudspeakers will be louder than cheers later in the game.

Three fans who drove from Kentucky to the game will get beery happy in the bar across the street and never see the game.

The box seats, where Detroit society reigns, will

be filled last.

The governor and the mayor will be booed with equal volume and intensity.

A 35-year-old businessman who played high school baseball with the visitors' superstar will try to find him and relive old times. He'll be rebuffed by ushers behind the dugout.

The press box will overflow with writers who won't return to the stadium for the rest of the season.

"TV Live at Noon" will interview the groundskeeper.

The first loud cheer will be for the fan who catches the first foul. He will be from Muskegon.

A rookie will get the home team's first hit. In two weeks, he'll be in the minors.

The lady wearing the whitest sweater will spill ketchup on it.

Four loud and abusive fans will threaten to sue when the concessionaire refuses to serve them more beer.

In the eighth inning, there will be an announcement in the press box that the press elevator is out of order.

After the game, the losing manager will say: "It's only one game. We'll be ready again tomorrow."

The winning manager will say: "It's only one game, but it's great to get off to a winning start."

A fan who's seen 52 straight openers will leave the park, saying, "It's still fun. There's nothing like Opening Day."

Originally printed on April 8, 1991

Get Out of My Bed and We've Got a Deal

JOHN COLLIER/Detroit Free Press

Whether it was going in for a hard slide at home or saving the Stanley Cup from would-be assailants, Kirk Gibson always went the extra mile.

Gibby saved the Cup from engraved danger

Did you know that a World Series hero saved the Stanley Cup?

In 1997, just a couple of weeks after the Wings had captured the Cup, Kirk Gibson saved it from destruction.

Yes, the savior was Gibson, the man who hit the most famous home run in Dodgers history and who climaxed the Tigers' 1984 Series triumph with two home runs in the final game against San Diego.

It all began with a quiet dinner party that Steve Yzerman held for 13 couples on a large boat. The center of attention was the Stanley Cup; all the guests had to inspect it and admire it.

As usual, the NHL had sent a representative to guard the Cup. Gibby was there, too.

Later in the evening, the celebration moved to a home in Grosse Pointe. Yzerman, weary from all the activities since winning the Cup, had left the group and gone to bed.

Before he retired, Stevie told the NHL's Cup guardian: "You've had a long, tough day. This is a good group. The Cup is safe.

"Why don't you go home and get some rest?"

The Cup man did as directed.

Later, the party began to get more spirited, and some of the celebrators began to get ideas.

"Hey, let's engrave our names on the Cup. We can

do it on the bottom," one of them suggested.

They proceeded to unscrew the bottom of the Cup, only to discover a second bottom that could not be unscrewed because it was riveted.

Now things were getting serious. Somebody headed for the garage and returned with an electric drill.

This is when Gibson entered the scene. He confronted the celebrators.

"Hold it, guys!" he said. "You can't do this. Let's calm down. Forget about the drill. Forget about engraving. Instead, let's all have a toast from the Cup."

There was resistance.

Some other Wings were there, and they joined Kirk in his efforts to restore sanity. The would-be engravers retreated, put down the drill, and the party returned to normal.

Gibby and the others took the Cup and put it to bed with Yzerman. The Captain would awake with it in the morning.

The Cup would not be engraved with names of overzealous fans.

The Stanley Cup has survived many adventures and will experience many more.

This time, it was saved by a World Series hero.

Originally printed on June 18, 1998

The real Crash makes it with a bang

S ometimes, names become famous in a round-about way. Take the case of Crash Davis. The great baseball movie "Bill Durham" made that name famous. The zany minor leaguer, played by Kevin Costner, touched moviegoers and baseball fans in a special way.

The director of "Bull Durham" was Ron Shelton, a former infielder in the Baltimore Orioles' organization. Shelton had promised his dad that if he didn't make the majors by age 26, he would retire. He reached Rochester, N.Y., one step from the big-league Orioles.

"After that season," Ron said, "I was 26 and I knew I wasn't going to be a major leaguer. So I quit."

Shelton played on a championship team that year with Don Baylor, Johnny Oates and Bobby Grich. Oates told me that Ron was a great guy to have around, but was a backup for Grich.

"That's the problem that dogged Shelton throughout his career in the Baltimore system," Oates said. "Wherever he played, Grich was always there ahead of him."

After the 1971 season, the Orioles sold Shelton's contract to the Tigers, who wanted him for Toledo. Even though he was not backing up Grich anymore, Ron felt he had reached the end of the trail.

Even after Shelton established himself as a top

screenwriter and director, he maintained his devotion to baseball. His idea of a good time is thumbing through the Baseball Encyclopedia.

"When I was writing 'Bull Durham,'" he said, "I was looking for a name for my hero. I dug through the Carolina League record book and saw that the league record for doubles was 52, set by Crash Davis.

"What a great name for a ballplayer," I told myself. So I used it for the Costner role."

Toward the end of Shelton's shooting of "Bull Durham," one of his assistants came to him and said: "Ron, there's a man named Crash Davis here. He is insisting on seeing you."

So Shelton met the real Crash Davis. He swallowed hard and ventured: "Are you going to sue me for using your name in the movie?"

"No," Davis told him. "I won't sue you. But tell me — in the movie, do I get the girl?"

"You sure do, Mr. Davis," Shelton answered. "Not only do you get the girl, but she is the ultimate catch — Susan Sarandon."

Crash told Shelton that before he set that record for doubles with the Durham Bulls, he had been with Connie Mack's Athletics. His real name was Lawrence Columbus Davis. He played baseball at Duke under Jack Coombs and was an infielder with the Athletics in 1940-42.

Davis and Shelton became friends. When Shelton was casting a later film, "Cobb," he chose Crash to play the role of Tigers great Sam Crawford.

Originally printed on April 22, 1994

Ike's secret changed the course of history

It was Dwight Eisenhower's lifelong secret that he was the only professional baseball player among all the U.S. presidents. Had he not kept that secret in his West Point days, he would not have become president and the great military leader of World War II.

Dwight's first baseball experience came as a centerfielder for his Abilene, Kan., high school team. In 1911, in his first year at West Point, he played both baseball and football. The next fall, playing football for Army against Carlisle, Ike injured his knee and never again played football.

He continued with baseball but failed to make the team at West Point.

"Not making that Army team was one of the great disappointments of my life," Ike once said.

Now about that secret of Ike's. Before he even went to college, he had played professionally.

"I needed money to go to college," he said, "and the best way to get it was to play pro baseball. I didn't do very well at it, but playing pro ball did help me with my financial problems."

While still at West Point, Eisenhower played professional ball one summer in the Kansas State league under the name of Wilson.

Many college athletes in those days competed in pro sports under assumed names — even though the NCAA rules forbade such activity and the penalties were stiff. There were even more serious rules at West Point, where student-athletes had to sign a pledge that they had never competed in pro sports. Ike signed that pledge — a clear violation of the West Point honor code. Any cadet who violated the honor code was expelled.

An expelled Eisenhower might have changed the course of world history. Ike would never have become a general. There would have been no Eisenhower, the World War II hero, and he would never have become president of the United States.

In their excellent book, "Baseball: The President's Game," William B. Mead and Paul Dickson point out that Ike revealed that he played pro ball when interviewed in June 1945, after his return from Europe. However, after that year, he became much more careful about his secret and instructed his staff to maintain a silence about his baseball career.

The authors write that "playing a few professional ballgames certainly was no sin. But under the rules of the day, it could cost Dwight David Eisenhower his place in history."

Originally printed on May 7, 1993

Get out of my bed and we've got a deal

You've heard the old expression, "Politics makes strange bedfellows." A baseball trade can also make strange bedfellows.

Emil (Buzzie) Bavasi told me this one.

For many years, Buzzie was general manager for the Dodgers and later the Angels. This story happened when Buzzie was with the Dodgers in Brooklyn.

John Quinn was general manager of the Milwaukee Brewers, and he coveted Dodgers outfielder Andy Pafko. Andy, who grew up in Wisconsin, was a great favorite there. He had eight-plus outstanding years with the Cubs and had finished a year and a half with Brooklyn.

Quinn came to the 1952 winter baseball meetings in Columbus, Ohio, determined to acquire Pafko from Brooklyn. He hounded Bavasi throughout the convention.

After a tiresome day, Bavasi was getting ready for bed when he answered a knock on his door and found Quinn standing outside.

"We've got to talk about Pafko," Quinn told Buzzie.

"Come on in," Bavasi said. "I'm getting ready for bed."

"I'll give you $100,000 for Pafko," Quinn said.

"No deal," Bavasi said.

"How about $125,000?"

"Not enough."

Bavasi went to the bathroom, brushed his teeth. Then he put on his pajamas.

"I'll give you $150,000," Quinn told him.

"No, John," Buzzie said. "I need a player. Besides, I'm going to bed."

Bavasi hopped in the bed. Quinn persisted. He began to shed his clothes.

"Move over," he told Bavasi. "I'm in this bed with you until I get Pafko."

"All right, John," Buzzie said. "You give me $150,000, Roy Hartsfield, get out of my bed, and we've got a deal."

Pafko went to Milwaukee and stayed there for seven seasons. He appeared in World Series with the Braves in 1957 and '58.

Hartsfield, the player Bavasi demanded, was less successful. He never appeared in a big-league game with the Dodgers, but played three seasons with the Boston Braves. Hartsfield became the first manager in Toronto history, managing the Jays from their start in 1977 through three seasons.

But Hartsfield and Pafko proved that baseball trades, like politics, make strange bedfellows.

Originally printed on July 13, 1991

Hammer's first hit was with the A's

H is name was Stanley Burrell. He used to bring us the lineups in the radio booth at Oakland County Coliseum. They called him Hammer because he looked like Henry (Hammerin' Hank) Aaron. He wore a green and gold baseball cap with VP on it.

Indeed, Athletics owner Charlie Finley even introduced Stanley as his vice president at a press conference. Finley had discovered Burrell in the Coliseum parking lot, pitching pennies and dancing around with his teenage pals. Stanley's brothers worked in the A's clubhouse, so he was always hanging around.

When Stanley joined forces with Finley, the Oakland franchise was in bad condition. The team had slipped in the standings, and Finley's visits became less frequent. He continued to run the Athletics and his insurance company from Chicago.

Only a few relatives remained in Oakland to man the front office. There were no full-time scouts. And the team's radio rights were passed off to a small University of California radio station in Berkeley.

At $7.50 a game, Stanley Burrell became a part of this scene. When Finley needed to follow the A's games from Chicago, Stanley phoned him the play-by-play. The Hammer even talked himself into the radio booth a couple of times and did his own play-by-play. That career came to an abrupt halt when the station's general manager tuned on his car radio.

"Get that kid off the air!" he ordered.

Hammer had other ideas of self-promotion. He went to Frank Cienscyk, the A's equipment manager, and told him, "Mr. Finley wants me in an A's uniform with a hammer on the back."

"When Charlie calls me and tells me that, you'll have the uniform," Cienscyk told him.

The players looked on Stanley as a spy. "It was scary," said Steve McCatty, a Troy native pitching for the A's at that time.

"We'd look up at the press box, see Hammer on the phone, and realize that our careers might depend on what a teenage kid was telling Finley back in Chicago."

Fast-forward to 1990.

It's Game 3 of the AL playoffs. On the mound to throw out the ceremonial first pitch is Stanley Burrell, the Hammer. Except now he's known as M. C. Hammer, music superstar.

He's M. C. Hammer, Grammy winner, seller of seven million albums, rap artist and multimillionaire.

But he couldn't have made it to the cover of Rolling Stone without the A's. First Finley discovered him, then two Oakland players provided him with seed money for his record company.

Stanley Burrell, the A's former vice president, was on top of the world.

Originally printed on June 29, 1991

He pitched baseballs; she pitched raisins

The best-looking women in town are always the wives of the baseball stars — you can bet on that. So it should come as no surprise that ballplayers' wives have often modeled and appeared in commercials.

But long before the advent of the TV commercial, the Tigers had a handsome pitcher whose wife not only was a model — she was the Sun-Maid Raisin Girl. If you saw a Sun-Maid Raisin box — in New York or Boston or Berlin or Istanbul — the face on that box belonged to this lady.

The pitcher was Earl Whitehill, and his wife was named Violet.

Violet had been a chorus girl on Broadway (where she met Earl) and Miss California. As the Sun-Maid Raisin girl, she toured the United States and even met President Woodrow Wilson.

I had heard for many years that Earl Whitehill's wife had been the Sun-Maid Raisin girl, but it was one of those pieces of trivia that floated around, and nobody could ever trace the truth of it. Then one night in Anaheim, the Tigers were playing the Angels, and into our radio booth walked Vince Desmond, then the Tigers' traveling secretary.

"I left some tickets for Mrs. Earl Whitehill tonight," he told me. "She is coming to the game with Tommy Bridges' widow. They both work in a nursing home near Anaheim."

I asked Vince to go to Mrs. Whitehill's seat and ask whether she really was the Sun-Maid Raisin girl. He came back an inning later with the news that Violet's picture was indeed the one we had seen on the Sun-Maid Raisin box. But, he added, there had been other Sun-Maid Raisin girls. Mrs. Whitehill had been pictured on the boxes for many years. But two or three ladies had followed her.

What about her ball-playing husband? Earl Whitehill was one of the most handsome major-leaguers. He never worked as a model, but he was a fine left-handed pitcher, winning 218 games over his 17-year career. Earl started in the majors with the Tigers and pitched for them from 1923 until he was traded to Washington after the '32 season. In 1933, Whitehill pitched the Senators to a pennant with 22 wins and shut out the Giants in the World Series for Washington's only win against the New Yorkers. In the late '30s, he pitched for Cleveland and for the Cubs.

Whitehill was tough and never backed down. Once he protested an umpire's decision by heaving the ump's whisk broom over the grandstand. Another time after a tough loss, he locked himself in his hotel room and wouldn't let his roommate in.

Off the field, Earl was handsome, cultured and polished. He and Violet were quite a couple.

And the record book tells us Whitehill was quite a pitcher.

Originally printed on June 8, 1991

These rules were made to be broken

I want to get something off my chest about the baseball scoring rules. Several times I've mentioned some of these objections on my broadcasts. But now I have a chance to object in more detail.

One of my pet peeves is giving an assist to a fielder when a batter or runner is not retired. Rule 10.11 says: "An assist shall be credited to each fielder who throws or deflects a batted or thrown ball in such a way that a putout results, or would have resulted except for a subsequent error by any fielder."

Let's take an example. The batter hits a grounder to the second baseman. He throws to first, and the first baseman drops the ball for an error. The batter is safe. Yet the second baseman gets an assist.

Why an assist? What did he assist in doing? The batter was safe, not out.

In football, if a quarterback's pass is dropped, the quarterback is not credited with a completion. If a basketball player passes to a teammate who misses a lay-up, he doesn't get an assist. In baseball, it always has been backward, and I don't understand it.

Here's another peeve. Rule 10.08 says: "A runner shall be charged as 'caught stealing' if he is put out, or would have been put out by an errorless play when he tries to steal."

Example: Runner on first breaks for second. Catcher throws the ball to the shortstop, who drops the ball. The runner is charged "caught stealing."

Does that make sense? Of course not. How can a runner be caught stealing when he is safe? It would be just as logical to say a batter would have hit a home run if the outfielder hadn't caught the ball. I don't get it. The man is standing on second, but the record book says he is caught stealing.

Another peeve. This one is not directly connected with scoring. Nevertheless, it defies logic in the same way as my other two peeves.

Look in any record book at a list of no-hit games. Most of them went nine innings, and logically enough the pitcher did not allow the opponent a hit. That's a no-hitter. Right? Right. Now, look at the entries when a game went longer than 10 innings. There have been a few 10-inning games in which a pitcher turned back the opposition without a hit. But also in those lists are extra-inning games designated as no-hitters that are not really no-hitters. In those games the opponents had hits in the extra innings.

For instance, Harvey Haddix's classic. Here's the way it reads in the record book:

"1959. Haddix, Harvey Jr., Pitt (at) Mil May 26 (0-1) (hit in 13th: lost)."

That was a great performance. But to me it is not a no-hitter. To give Haddix a no-hitter is like saying Walt Terrell pitched a shutout when Chicago scored a run in the 11th and beat him, 1-0.

In other words, don't award any player anything

until the game is over. Don't defy the final score.

Editor's note: Since this column was printed on May 18, 1991, the commissioner's office has sided with Ernie on feats such as Haddix's and disallowed them as no-hitters.

Ernie Harwell

Closer

Some sure signs of a book signing

The world of book selling demands that people who write books be subjected to a tribal custom of signing their books in bookstores across the country. Many authors can't withstand the ordeal. They don't want to fight the fatigue of flying from city to city, appearing on radio and TV, and meeting the public.

I enjoy signing books. It's hard work, but I'm privileged to meet some great people face-to-face. Many are Tigers fans or just baseball fans. Some are people who love books and just want to be friendly. On radio and TV, you never get a chance to know who is out there tuned in to you. When you sign books, you get to meet these folks face-to-face.

Through the years, I have compiled a list of things that are bound to happen at book signings.

Wherever you park at the mall will be the farthest distance from the store where you are signing. ... The first person in line will tell you he has been waiting for over an hour. ... The sign announcing your appearance will be smaller than a bikini. ... One long-winded customer will hold up the line while he tells you his grandfather knew Ty Cobb.

Several ladies taking their lunch stroll will look at the line and ask each other, "Who's that old guy? And why would anybody line up for his autograph?" ... Twenty-eight people couldn't get to the bookstore. They have phoned and asked for autographed books. ... Somebody will volunteer to take you to lunch at a restaurant in the mall. ...

You'll be asked to dedicate books to people with difficult and similar names. There will always be Ellen, Eileen, Aileen, Shawn or Sean. ... Even a name like John can sometimes be spelled Jon. ... One person will bring you a book to sign and absent-mindedly leave the store without paying for it. ... One store worker will walk to the end of the mall to bring you a cup of coffee in a Styrofoam cup. ...

Several young parents will ask you to pose for a snapshot with their children. ... Others will want you to hold their baby for a photo. ... Some retirees will inquire if you served in World War II. ... You'll have to sign scraps of paper, balls, bats, photos, scrapbooks, T-shirts, caps and sometimes even the book you wrote.

If there is a lull in the signing, the store manager will request that you sign 15 or 20 books for future sales. ... If you can't, he'll ask you to stay after your appointed time and sign the extra books. ...

Your hand will hurt, and you'll be tired when the signing is done. ... But you'll discover that people who sell books are the most passionate and caring about their service. All are avid readers and love their work.

I'll see you at my next signing.

Originally printed on Sept. 30, 1994

Index

Index